The Way, The Truth and The Life

Teacher's Book 4

Authors

Sister Marcellina Cooney CP and Angela Edwards

Teachers' Enterprise in Religious Education Co. Ltd

Acknowledgements

Nihil obstat: Father Anton Cowan – Censor.
Imprimatur: The Most Rev. Vincent Nichols PhL, MA, Med, STL, Archbishop
                 of Westminster
                 Holy Thursday, 28 March 2013

The *Nihil obstat* and *Imprimatur* are a declaration that the books and contents of the CD ROM are free from doctrinal and moral error. It is not implied that those who have granted the *Nihil obstat* and the Imprimatur agree with the contents, opinions or statements expressed.

Design, compilation and format: Ian Curtis, First Sight Graphics, www.firstsightgraphics.com

Design and **Text copyright** © Sr. Marcellina Cooney CP

Picture research Sr. Marcellina Cooney CP and Ian Curtis.

Theological Adviser: Bryan Lobo SJ

Permission credits
Cover illustration: © Philip Hood, Arena Illustrations; © page 21 Mille Images Symboliques by Patrick Royer; © pages 22 & 24 Milles Images Bibliques Ancien Testament by Pierre-Michel Gambarelli & Mathias Grosclaude; © pages 37, 52-53 Mille Images Evangile by Jean-François Kieffer, Les Presses d'Ile de France; © C Jones/Shutterstock.com; © Holly Kuchera/Shutterstock.com; © file404/Shutterstock.com; © Redshinestudio/Shutterstock.com; © Nicemonkey/Shutterstock.com; © venimo/Shutterstock.com; © Vector/Shutterstock.com.

Every effort has been made to contact copyright holders of material used in this publication. Any omissions will be rectified in subsequent printing if notice is given to the Teachers' Enterprise in Religious Education Co. Ltd, 40 Duncan Terrace, London N2 8AL

Published by
Teachers' Enterprise in Religious Education Co. Ltd
40 Duncan Terrace, London N1 8AL

Printed in the UK by Geerings Print Ltd, www.geeringsprint.co.uk

Introduction

Welcome to the second revised edition of *The Way, the Truth & the Life* Teacher's Book 4. This forms part of the series developed for 3 – 14 year olds.

The Syllabus, Pupil's and Teacher's Books are based on the *Catechism of the Catholic Church* and the *Religious Education Curriculum Directory for Catholic Schools* published by the Bishops' Conference of England and Wales. The great strength of this series is its theological content linked in an imaginative way for todays 8-9 year olds.

In this revised edition pupils will study the Bible with particular reference to Abraham, Joseph, Moses and David in the Old Testament. In the New Testament the focus will be on the birth and mission of John the Baptist; the Nativity with links to the Trinity and the life and teaching of Jesus as truly God and as man truly human. In addition, pupils will study and reflect on the importantance of the passion, death, resurrection and ascension of Jesus.

The study of Pentecost will lead on to some of the lives of the early Christians and their teaching. The last module will focus on aspects of the Church.

These Books have been produced by the Teachers' Enterprise in Religious Education, that is, by teachers from different parts of the country working in a collaborative manner and pooling their expertise.

Fr. Bryan Lobo SJ has been a great source of encouragement to the teachers involved and I thank him warmly.

I trust that all who use this Teacher's Book, Pupil's Book, CD ROM and the supporting website www.tere.org, will be helped in a clear and direct way in the important task of enabling children to learn about the Catholic faith and to respond to its invitation with growing faith and generosity.

+Vincent Nichols

✠ **Vincent Nichols**
Archbishop of Westminster

Contents

Overview of Key Stage 2 Syllabus

	Autumn 1	Autumn 2	Spring 1	Spring 2	Summer 1	Summer 2
Year 3	3.1 The Christian Family	3.2 Mary, Mother of God	3.3 The Sacrament of Reconciliation	3.4 Celebrating the Mass	3.5 Celebrating Easter & Pentecost	3.6 Being a Christian
Year 4	4.1 The Bible	4.2 Trust in God	4.3 Jesus, the Teacher	4.4 Jesus, the Saviour	4.5 The Early Christians	4.6 The Church
Year 5	5.1 Gifts from God	5.2 The Commandments	5.3 Inspirational People	5.4 Reconciliation	5.5 Life in the Risen Jesus	5.6 People of Other Faiths
Year 6	6.1 The Kingdom of God	6.2 Justice	6.3 Jesus, the Bread of Life	6.4 Jesus, Son of God	6.5 The Work of the Apostles	6.6 Called to Serve

Contents of WTL CD ROM 4

Notes for Users

Overview of Syllabus

Links to the Religious Education Curriculum Directory

PPP: How to use the Catechism of the Catholic Church

4.1 The Bible
Power Point Presentations
Starter- The Bible
What is the Bible
Looking for Bible reference
God speaks to us in the Bible
The Bible and the Divine Office
Abraham
Sarah hears God's promise
Starter for Joseph
Joseph
Early life of Moses
Moses – Plagues & Exodus
Jewish Passover Today
David's Brothers

Smart Notebook
Introduction to the Bible – starter
The Bible: where would you find
Glossary

Worksheets
The Bible, a story about God's love
The Bible, finding your way around
Moses & the Exodus
David & Goliath
Sensational Headlines
God speaks to us in the Bible
How the Bible is used at Mass
The Hymn of Victory, Ex. 15

4.2 Trust in God
Power Point Presentations
Advent
Visit of the Wise Men
Flight into Egypt
Mystery of the Trinity
Mystery of the Incarnation

Smart Notebook
Trusting
Trusting in God
Zechariah
Joseph
Mary & Joseph
Being like Mary
What the birth of Jesus means for us
Glossary

Worksheets
Tom & Abigail
Mary visits Elizabeth
Mary's Song of Praise
Joseph – coat-hanger poem
Joseph trusts in God
Drama - Shepherds
Flight into Egypt
Christmas cards
Guided meditation – Trusting in God

4.3 Jesus the Teacher
Power Point Presentations
Jewish worship of God
The Twelve Disciples
Miracles of Jesus
The Sower
The Unfaithful Servant
Evaluating Behaviour
The Beatitudes

Smart Notebook
Helping others
Ripple effect
Parable of the Sower
Glossary

Worksheets
Jewish worship of God
Jesus shows us how to live
The Beatitudes

4.4 Jesus, the Saviour
Power Point Presentations
Lent
Jesus, human & divine
Jesus enters Jerusalem
Palm Sunday in Church
Meaning of the Last Supper
Meaning of the New Covenant
Stations of the Cross
Good Friday liturgy in Church
Why did Jesus die on a cross?
Mary, Mother of Jesus: sorrow and Joy
The Resurrection

Smart Notebook
Holy Week (1)
Holy Week (2)
Glossary

Worksheets
The donkey owner
Holy Week Diary
Passover – Last Supper – Eucharist
Peter lets Jesus down
The Paschal Mystery
Itsuo & Takeo

Audio Recording
The donkey owner

4.5 The Early Christians
Power Point Presentations
Peter's progress
Hot-seating Peter
Meaning of the Ascension
Stoning of Stephen
Conversion of Saul

Smart Notebook
Stephen & Saul
Peter & Paul
Glossary

Worksheets
Easter Liturgy
Prayers to the Holy Spirit
Stephen's speech
Peter & Paul
Map of Paul's journeys and notes
TV reporters and Paul

4.6 The Church
Power Point Presentations
Pope Francis I
Vestments for Mass
A Missionary Sister
Columban Sisters
St. Thérèse of Lisieux
Feast Days of Our Lady
Joyful Mysteries of the Rosary

Smart Notebook
The Church's Year
Glossary

Worksheets
Apostles' Creed
Our Parish Church
Prepare for our mission

Assessment
Levels of Attainment
Assessment Tasks
Guidance on Assessment Tasks

Collective Worship
A Morning Prayer
Trust in God
All Souls Day
Advent Service
Blessing the Christmas Crib
Blessing the Christmas Tree
Thoughts on the Resurrection

METHODOLOGY

Our starting point in presenting the religious content specified by the Religious Education Curriculum Directory should be **REVELATION**. God is always the initiator in the history of our creation and redemption; it is His revealing of Himself that makes classroom religious education possible. To begin with, Revelation ensures that we respect the revealed nature of Christian faith.

From Revelation, we move to **LIFE IN CHRIST,** in other words, we study and reflect on how God makes Himself known to us through Jesus, who is truly God and as a man, truly human.

Then, we focus on the **CHURCH** as the People of God. This leads to **CELEBRATION** – the liturgical and sacramental life of the Church, the moral life and the pursuit of holiness.

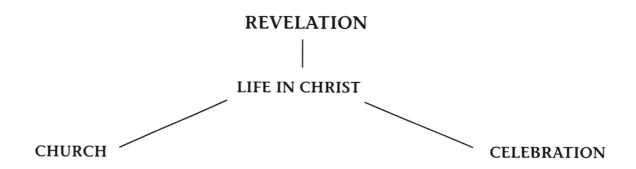

It is proposed that each of these areas should, as far as possible without artificial distortion, be covered in each book.

It is essential to make clear connections between the truths of faith and the pupils' own experiences of life. For many, it is only when they see the relevance to their own lives of what they are learning, that they become fully engaged in it.

However, the Gospel message always, at some point, takes the person beyond the scope of their own experience, challenging and transforming it. It is a message of a saving and transforming gift.

NOTES FOR USERS

The contents of this **Teacher's Book** and the companion **Pupil's Book 4** are based on the Key Stage 2 Syllabus, which is published as a separate document in this series. These resources cover all the essential content of the Religious Education Curriculum Directory of the Bishops' Conference of England and Wales.

The Syllabus incorporates two attainment targets: learning *about* the Catholic faith (AT1) and learning *from* Catholic faith (AT2). These are set out in the form of specific key learning objectives for each module and listed at the start of each section in both Teacher's and Pupil's Books. This syllabus can be used as a guide in curriculum planning. It is available from Redemptorist Publications and on our website www.tere.org

In the **Teacher's Book**, the key learning objectives are further developed for each module in the form of a Theological Introduction to enrich the teacher's understanding of the content they are about to teach. They are based mainly on the Catechism of the Catholic Church (CCC) and theological notes from Fr. Herbert Alphonso SJ. The **points for discussion, further activities, scripts for prayer** and **liturgies** together with **worksheets to photocopy** are all intended to complement the **Pupil's Book** and provide suggestions for differentiated work.

The section on **Assessment for Learning** offers guidance on different ways of monitoring pupils' progress. The Level Descriptors are based on the Levels of Attainment in Religious Education in Catholic Schools and Colleges, Bishops' Conference Department for Catholic Education & Formation.

The **CD ROM 4** offers a wide variety of Power Point Presentations, SMART notebooks, assessment tasks and worksheets. These ICT resources provide excellent pedagogical tools which can be adapted for pupils of all abilities and split classes.

Our **supporting website** www.tere.org offers a wide range of materials for teachers and interactive resources for pupils. Teachers are advised to check the suitability of all websites as the content may change at any time.

KEY to symbols and abbreviations in this Teacher's Book:

CCC = Catechism of the Catholic Church

RECD = Religious Education Curriculum Directory

 WS = worksheet

 PPP = Power Point Presentation on CD ROM

 SMART = Interactive electronic whiteboards

4.1 The Bible

Religious Education Curriculum Directory
"God is the author of Sacred Scripture. 'The divinely revealed realities, which are contained and presented in the text of Sacred Scripture, have been written down under the inspiration of the Holy Spirit'" (CCC 105).

Attainment Target 1: Learning *about* the Catholic faith.
Attainment Target 2: Learning *from* the Catholic faith.

Key Learning Objectives

- Know that the Bible is an account of God's relationship with His people.
  - Reflect on how the Bible can help us.

- Know that God calls Abraham.
  - Think about the challenges and blessings Abraham experienced.

- Know about God's call to Joseph.
  - Reflect on God's plan for him.

- Know about God's call to Moses.
  - Reflect on what we can learn from his experience.

- Know that David was chosen by God.
  - Reflect on David's trust in God.

- Know that God speaks to us in the Bible.
  - Reflect on some things God tells us.

Theological Notes

Q. How do we know that the Bible is the inspired word of God?
"God inspired the human authors of the sacred books. 'To compose the sacred books, God chose certain men who, all the while He employed them in this task, made full use of their own faculties and powers so that, though he acted in them and by them, it was as true authors that they consigned to writing whatever he wanted written, and no more' (CCC 106).

The inspired books teach the truth. 'Since therefore all that the inspired authors or sacred writers affirm should be regarded as affirmed by the Holy Spirit, we must acknowledge that the books of Scripture firmly, faithfully, and without error teach that truth which God, for the sake of our salvation, wished to see confided to the Sacred Scriptures'" (CCC 107).

Q. How were the Gospels written?

The Canon of Scripture - "In keeping with the Lord's command, the Gospel was handed on in two ways:

orally 'by the apostles who handed on, by the spoken word of their preaching, by the example they gave, by the institutions they established, what they themselves had received – whether from the lips of Christ, from his way of life and his works, or whether they had learned it at the promptings of the Holy Spirit;'

in writing 'by those apostles and other men associated with the apostles who, under the inspiration of the same Holy Spirit, committed the message of salvation to writing'" (CCC 76).

Q. What are the three stages in the formation of the Gospels?

1. *The Life and teaching of Jesus.* The Church holds firmly that the four Gospels, 'whose historicity she unhesitatingly affirms, faithfully hand on what Jesus, the Son of God, while he lived among men (people), really did and taught for their eternal salvation, until the day when he was taken up.'

2. *The Oral Tradition.* 'For, after the ascension of the Lord, the apostles handed on to their hearers what he had said and done, but with that fuller understanding which they, instructed by the glorious events of Christ and enlightened by the Spirit of truth, now enjoyed.

3. *The written Gospels.* 'The sacred authors, in writing the four Gospels, selected certain of the many elements which had been handed on, either orally or already in written form (CCC 126).

Q. Why did God choose Abraham?

"In order to gather together scattered humanity God calls Abram from his country, his kindred and his father's house, and makes him Abraham, that is, 'the father of a multitude of nations'. 'In you all the nations of the earth shall be blessed'" (CCC 59).

"The people descended from Abraham would be the trustee of the promise made to the patriarchs, the chosen people, called to prepare for that day when God would gather all His children into the unity of the Church. They would be the root on to which the Gentiles would be grafted, once they came to believe" (CCC 62).

"Israel is the priestly people of God, 'called by the name of the Lord', and 'the first to hear the word of God', the people of 'elder brethren' in the faith of Abraham" (CCC63).

"God chose Abraham and made a covenant with him and his descendants. By the covenant God formed His people and revealed His law to them through Moses. Through the prophets, He prepared them to accept the salvation destined for all humanity" (CCC 72).

Additional Theological Notes

Brief history of Salvation

From the start, God revealed Himself to our first parents Adam and Eve, as the Book of Genesis tells us; He invited them to an intimate communion with himself, clothing them with the splendid dignity of original grace and justice. Even when they disobeyed God and, through sin, lost their friendship with God, He did not abandon our first parents to the powers of death; soon after their fall He promised the Redeemer, and took personal care of them and their offspring. Again and again He offered a covenant to human beings, and through the prophets taught them to hope for salvation.

Thus, when the unity of the human race was threatened and began to be destroyed by sin, God sought in every way to save humankind in His love. After the deluge God made an alliance with Noah to express His will to save "all nations". Even so, the pride and arrogance of selfish humanity concurred, through the construction of the Tower of Babel, to build its own kind of unity in opposition to, and frustration of, God's loving plan and design. But God's faithful love relentlessly pursued the pedagogical carrying out of His design of love; to bring together into unity the human race divided and dispersed through the sinful pride and selfishness of humankind.

God chose Abraham, calling him out of his own country, his father's house and parentage, to make of him "the father of a multitude of peoples", in whom all the nations of the earth would be blessed. This alliance which God made with Abraham and confirmed with his descendants Isaac and Jacob – the Patriarchs, as all three are called – would make of the people descending from them the depository of the promises made to these patriarchs; this people would be known as "the people of the election", that is, "the chosen people", called by God to prepare the reassembling one day in the unity of the Church all the scattered children of God, brought together as one family by the redeeming work and mission of Jesus Christ.

In this wondrous pedagogical manner of faithfully carrying out His loving design, God made of Abraham and his descendants a people to whom He revealed His Law through Moses. He patiently prepared his chosen people, right through the period of the Kings – especially King David, the King after God's own heart – and that of the prophets, to welcome the salvation He had planned, in love, for all humanity.

Indeed, God revealed Himself finally, fully and definitively through and in His Son Jesus Christ, in whom He sealed His final alliance for all time. Jesus Christ is the final and definitive word of God the Father: in **him** all God's revelation is completely contained and summed up, so that, after him, there is and will be no further revelation (cf. Heb. 1:1-2).

God calls Moses

Moses was tending the flock of sheep of his father-in-law Jethro. As he was leading the sheep into the wilderness, he came to the mountain of God, Horeb. There God appeared to him in the burning bush. What Moses saw was the bush aflame; but the bush, he noticed, was not being consumed by the flames. So Moses became curious; it is God's own Word that calls attention to Moses' curiosity. Wanting to understand and grasp this strange phenomenon, he started making a tour of the bush, as it were, to 'master' this phenomenon. Then it was that God spoke out of the bush: "Moses! Moses! Do not come near, stand away from here: this is holy ground. Take off your shoes; your sandals from your feet, for you are standing on holy ground. I am God: the God of your father Abraham, the God of Isaac and the God of Jacob".

In other words, God is saying to Moses: "The only position for you is face-down on the ground, prostrate before me, for I am God – the God of Abraham, of Isaac and of Jacob". And it is not until Moses has moved away from that holy ground and acknowledged God as God (cf. Ex. 3:6), that he will receive effectively his call and mission from God to be, in God's name, the liberator of God's people from slavery and oppression in Egypt.

"I have heard", says God to Moses, "the cry of the people in Egypt, the people enslaved and oppressed. I am sending you to the King of Egypt, to Pharaoh, to ask him to release my people and let them go." We should note Moses' reaction. "Who am I", he says to God, "that I should go to Pharaoh and tell him to let the people go?" "Who am I? I know **you** are God, the God of my fathers Abraham, Isaac and Jacob; I have acknowledged **you** as such. But who am I?" Then it is that God says: "I will be with you. Go!" We would do well to pay close attention to these words, which will continually and unfailingly recur in every call and vocation, after God who calls has been acknowledged and worshipped as God: "Do not be afraid, I will be with you. I **am** with you."

The characteristic of God right through the revelation of the Old Testament is **God's faithful love**: He is and remains always, relentlessly so, the God of covenant love, the God who remains unfailingly faithful to His covenant of merciful, forgiving, reconciling and transforming love.

Herbert Alphonso SJ

4.1 The Bible

**Know that the Bible is an account of God's relationship with His people.
Reflect on how the Bible can help us.**

What is the Bible?

Starting point
Ask the pupils what they know about the Bible. What stories do they already know? What is their favourite story? Why?

SMART page: Introduction - **The Bible** starter (CD ROM).

Display: It will help to have a new copy of the Bible on a display table with a picture or statue of Jesus and some prayer cards, for example,

> **Prayer in the morning**
> *Dear God*
> *Before I start my work today*
> *Let me not forget to pray.*
> *Guide me; help me in all I do*
> *so that I can always be with you.*

> **Prayer for help**
> *God in heaven hear my prayer,*
> *keep me in thy loving care.*
> *Be my guide in all I do,*
> *Bless all those who love me too.*

> **God our Father,**
> *You call each of us by name,*
> *and you treasure each of us individually.*
> *Inspire us to respect and value*
> *each person who comes into our lives this day. Amen.*

PPP: What is the Bible? (CD ROM)

PPP: Looking for a Bible reference. (CD ROM)

Worksheet: The Bible: Finding your way around

SMART: Where would you find the following events? (CD ROM)
SMART: Fill in the missing word (CD ROM)

Plenary activity
  a) How would you explain what the Bible is to someone who knows nothing about it?
  b) Can you explain why the Bible is important?

God calls Abraham

> Know that God calls Abraham.
> Think about the challenges and blessings Abraham experienced.

God's Plan

Starting point

Ask if any of the children have had to leave their own country or move house, leaving behind all their friends.

- What was it like? Were they worried? Why?
- Did they know what to expect in the new country or home?
- What was most difficult about it?
- What did they miss most of all when they left home?

Explain

We are now going to learn how God makes Himself known and how He begins to build a relationship of faith and friendship with the people He chooses, for example Abraham. Use Pupils' Book to explain what happened.

Pupil's Book page 10
Discuss Activity 1: What does the story of Abraham tell us about:

- a) God *(Possible answers – God takes the initiative, He is the one who called Abraham; God keeps His promises and He is full of surprises).*
- b) Abraham *(He had great faith and trust in God)*
- c) Sarah *(She was very human, e.g. laughed when she was told she was going to have a baby; but she was honest and loyal to Abraham).*

PPP: Abraham (CD ROM)

PPP: Sarah hears God's promise (CD ROM)

Discuss

- How do you think Sarah felt when Abraham first told her what God had asked him to do?
- How would you have felt?
- Was Abraham wise to obey God? Why? Why not?
- What promises did God make to Abraham?
- Was it easy to believe that these promises would come true? Why? Why not?
- The first lesson that God was teaching Abraham was to have faith in Him and to trust Him. How difficult do you think this was?
- What helps you to trust in God? Do you find it easy?

Plenary activity - In what way did God keep His promise to Abraham and Sarah?

Joseph

Know about God's call to Joseph.
Reflect on God's plan for him.

Joseph

Background information

Jacob, the son of Isaac, married Rachel and had twelve sons. Jacob favoured and loved his son Joseph. This made Joseph's brothers jealous and cruel towards him. One night, Joseph dreamt that he and his brothers were binding sheaves of corn in a field and that his brothers' sheaves bowed down to his sheaf. Another night, he dreamt that the sun, the moon and eleven stars bowed before him.

Facts about Joseph: seventeen years old; a dreamer; the favourite son of his father who gave him a beautiful coat.

 PPP: Starting point for Joseph – God helps in mysterious ways
When we pray to God and ask for His help, it does not mean that we will automatically receive an answer. God will answer - but frequently, it is in His time not ours. God works in mysterious ways. God was looking after Joseph to make sure that everything would work out well in the end.

 PPP 'Joseph' (CD ROM)

[It is essential to use the text in the Pupil's Book before the following discussion.]

Discussion pointers (PPP 'Joseph' has the following questions and more with the appropriate illustrations)

- Why do you think the brothers became envious of Joseph?
- Why do you think Joseph told his brothers about his dreams?
- Do you think he was boasting or was he just sharing what had happened?
- What were the consequences?
- Why did the brothers throw him into the pit?
- What did they do with his coat? Why?
- Why did the brothers lie to their father?
- What do you think their conscience was telling them to do?
- Who took Joseph to Egypt?
- What happened when he got there?
- Why did Joseph end up in prison?

- What happened in prison?
- In what way did he help the other prisoners?
- Why did Pharaoh send for Joseph?
- How did Joseph help Pharaoh?
- In what way do you think God was helping Joseph?
- Think back to Joseph's dreams – did they come true?
- What happened?
- Who sent Joseph's brothers to Egypt?
- Did they recognise Joseph?
- How do you think Joseph felt when he saw his brothers again?
- How do you think the brothers felt when they found Joseph alive and in a powerful position?

Pause to Reflect
- Think of all that happened to Joseph. In what ways was God looking after him?
- In what ways did evil turn to good – think about all the things Joseph was able to do to help others.

Activity 2 page 14
Some prompt questions for Jacob to ask:
- Why did you put Joseph in the well?
- He was only a silly boy, why did you want to kill him?
- Why did you tell me a lie?
- What did your conscience tell you to do?
- How do you think I felt when I thought Joseph was dead?
- Have you no feelings for me?
- How are you now going to show Joseph that you are truly sorry?

Additional activity
Work in pairs. One of you is Joseph and the other Jacob.
Imagine the conversation you had when you finally met after so many years.

SMART notebook: Glossary

Plenary activity
Write down what you think is the most important thing you have learnt about Joseph.

God calls Moses

Know about God's call to Moses.
Reflect on what we can learn from his experience.

Life in Egypt

 Starting point: A summary of life in Egypt is in the Pupil's Book but more detail of Moses as a baby is in Pupil's Book 2 and on the CD ROM.

 PPP: **Early life of Moses** to his escape to Midian.

Additional information to share with pupils

The account of the Exodus is one of the greatest events in the history of the Israelites. It explains how people suffered because of very harsh treatment by Pharaoh. These poor people put their faith in God. Pharaoh had been warned many times by Moses that God wanted His people to be set free. Pharaoh would not listen. He hardened his heart against God's will.

At last, Pharaoh gave the Israelites permission to leave but they had only just gone when he changed his mind and sent his army after them. Guided by a pillar of cloud by day and fire by night, the Israelites reached the Red Sea. At God's command, Moses raised his staff and the sea divided and allowed them to escape.

God showed that no power on earth, no matter how great, could stand against Him.

 Worksheet: Moses and the Exodus page 22.

 PPP: **Moses – Plagues and Exodus**
PPP: **Jewish Passover today**

How do Jews celebrate the Passover today?

The Passover is one of the most important religious festivals in the Jewish calendar. Jews celebrate the Feast of Passover (*Pesach* in Hebrew) to commemorate the liberation of the Children of Israel who were led out of Egypt by Moses. Details are available on the BBC Learning Zone.

 Listen to the story of the Passover
http://www.bbc.co.uk/religion/religions/judaism
(scroll down to the end of the page to find the YouTube link)

www.topmarks.co.uk/judaism/moses/moses1.htm Moses

David is chosen by God

Know that David was chosen by God.
Reflect on David's trust in God.

David is anointed King

 Starting point: Ask the pupils what qualities they think people look for when they want to choose someone for important tasks. *(For example, experience, qualifications, ability to inspire others).*

Explain that you are now going to find out some of the qualities God looks for in a person He chooses.

 PPP: David's brothers – explains why God chose David and how God has plans for each person. (CD ROM)

 Additional activities
1. Discuss
   a) Was King Saul wise to let David fight Goliath? Give reasons.
   b) What do you think helped King Saul to decide what to do?
   c) What do you think David's brothers expected to happen?
   d) If you had been there what advice would you have given to King Saul?

 2. **Worksheet:** David and Goliath (TB p. 24-25)

3. Why do you think the account of David and Goliath should be included in a book of Bible Stories for children?

www.tere.org Interactive Section, Key Stage 2 click on 'Trails' for 'David & Goliath', 'Moses & Exodus' and the 'Bible' reference.

http://www.ainglkiss.com/bibst/mos1htm OT Stories

Google search: David – Free Power Points for Church, Bible Study, Bible Stories.

Note: Teachers need to check websites and supervise pupils using them as the content frequently changes. The above are only suggestions and TERE takes no responsibility for their use.

God Speaks to Us

Know that God speaks to us in the Bible.
Reflect on some things God tells us.

God speaks to us in the Bible

 Starting point: Think about the places where you might see a Bible, or hear one being read. Is there a Bible in your home? Does anyone have their own Bible?

Explain
We believe that the Bible is God's Word. The Bible is God speaking to us. He has spoken to people all down the ages and for a long, long period up to when Jesus became man.

The Bible is used at Mass.
One important part of the Mass is called the '**Liturgy of the Word**'.
On Sundays, we listen to four readings from the Bible.
The first one is from the Old Testament. It could be about Abraham, Joseph, Moses, David or one of the prophets. Then there is a psalm from the Old Testament. A psalm is a kind of hymn or prayer.

There is also a reading from the New Testament; perhaps something that happened in the early Church, or maybe part of a letter that St Peter or St Paul wrote to explain something. After that, we have the most important reading from the Bible – the Gospel reading.

 Additional activity
Choose one or two of the quotations from the Bible that you think will help you most of all. Use them to make a 'Prayer Card' to keep at home.

Meditation *(Draw the blinds and light a candle. Begin by playing some music very softly to help the pupils become still – then turn off the music and read the quotations in the Pupil's Book page 22 or alternatively use the PPP on CD ROM).*

 PPP: Meditation quotations: **God speaks to us in the Bible.**
When you are ready explain to the pupils: we are now going to ask God to speak to each one of us so we must think carefully about His words. At the end play the music again. Then invite pupils to share which quotation helped them most of all.

 Worksheet: How the Bible is used at Mass (CD ROM).

 PPP: How the Bible is used for the Divine Office.

How the Bible is used at Mass

Liturgy of the Word

One important part of the Mass is called the 'Liturgy of the Word'. We believe that the Bible is God's Word. The Bible is God speaking to us. He has spoken to us all down the ages and for a long, long period up to when Jesus became man.

On Sundays, we listen to four readings from the Bible.
The first one is usually from the Old Testament. It could be about Abraham, Joseph, Moses, David or one of the prophets. Then there is a psalm from the Old Testament. A psalm is a kind of hymn or prayer.

The second reading is from the New Testament; perhaps something that happened in the early Church, or maybe part of a letter that St Peter or St Paul wrote to explain something.

After that, we have the most important reading from the Bible – the Gospel reading. To show how important it is to listen to what Jesus did and said:

- we stand up;
- the Altar servers bring the candles to each side of the Book of the Gospels;
- we sing the Alleluia (except in Lent);
- the priest kisses the Book of the Gospels before he reads.
- we make three small signs of the cross on:
  - our forehead to show we will think about the Gospel;
  - our lips to show we will share it with others;
  - our chest to show we will keep the words of Jesus in our hearts.

Activity

a) Choose one reading from the Old Testament.
b) In your own words, write a short account of this reading.
c) Explain how this reading could be used at Mass.
d) What do you think the priest might say in his homily about it?
   (Think about why the reading is important and who it might help).

Moses and the Exodus

One day, God spoke to **Moses** and asked him to go to Pharaoh, the king to ask him to free the Israelites because they were being treated very badly. Moses did not think he could do it, but God assured him that He would be with him.

So Moses went along to the King of Egypt – Pharaoh – and demanded that he let his people go. Now, this was quite something. For one thing, usually no one could get within a hundred metres of Pharaoh but – well, Moses was determined and, to give him his due, he succeeded. However, the chances of Pharaoh releasing the Israelites were remote. They were the Egyptians' slaves. They were used as labourers for building great cities.

Did Moses seriously think Pharaoh would agree? It would mean loss of cheap labour. Then, there was Moses' own problem. He was shy. He wasn't too good with words either. So he was hardly going to persuade Pharaoh to let the Israelites go, was he?

Well, that's when the plagues started, as we called them at the time. Each time Moses went along to Pharaoh with his demand, and each time Pharaoh refused. And so, God did everything possible to give Pharaoh a chance to change his mind.

First, the water in all the rivers and ponds and canals turned to blood! "Let the people go!" Moses demanded. "No!" replied Pharaoh. So along came another plague – frogs, millions upon millions of them, hopping all over the land. Then another – gnats; then flies, swarms of them everywhere. Nine times Moses went to Pharaoh and told him it was the will of God that the Israelites should be released. And each time, the King of the Egyptians refused. There were more plagues – all the cattle died, then everyone

developed boils, then there were huge hailstones, then swarms of locusts that ate all the crops; then the lights went out. Well, that's what it seemed like. There was darkness over the whole of Egypt for three whole days. No sun, no moon, no stars, nothing! Still Pharaoh remained stubborn.

"Very well!" said God. "I've given Pharaoh nine chances – nine warnings. This time he will let the Israelites go!"

God had given Pharaoh every chance possible, but still he would not do as God asked. So God told Moses to give his people these instructions:

"Get ready for a long journey. But before we go, we're going to eat a special meal: roast lamb with bitter herbs and unleavened bread (that is bread baked without yeast). The blood of the lamb needs to be sprinkled round our doors. Because tonight, God is going to pass over Egypt and all of the oldest children are going to die. But when He sees blood on the door-frames, He will pass over those houses because He will know that they belong to us – to the Israelites."

So that's what happened. God had tried everything before sending this, the tenth and most horrible plague. But Pharaoh refused to listen. And of course, whose son also died on that night? Well, you can imagine how he felt, can't you? "Get out of here!" he screamed at Moses. "Take your people and go! I never want to see any of you again. Your God is too powerful for me to resist any longer!"

The Israelites were ready. Their bags were packed, they had their walking shoes on their feet. They moved! Men, women and children, goats, sheep and cows, all headed out of Egypt – until they reached the Red Sea on Egypt's eastern border. But by this time, Pharaoh had had time to think about what had happened. He was still grieving for his dead son, but now he was angry too. "No! I want them back!" his voice echoed around his palace. "Get my chariot ready … and my whole army. We're going after them!"

Six hundred of his finest chariots thundered out of the city – followed by all his soldiers and horses. The Israelites on the shore of the Red Sea could see the dust rising on the horizon as they got nearer.

"What have you done, Moses?" they cried. "We were better off in Egypt. But now we're going to die!" That's when the next great miracle happened. "Raise your hand over the sea," God told Moses. Moses raised his hand over the water and the Red Sea divided. It wasn't a bridge. It wasn't a tunnel. It was a great dry route right through the middle of the sea.

"Come on!" someone shouted, and the Israelites surged forward, families and all their possessions, passing through the Red Sea, heading for freedom, for safety, for their own land as God had promised them. The Egyptians were close behind them, though. They saw them passing through the sea and Pharaoh ordered his army to follow. The chariots, the horses, the foot soldiers thundered into the channel and, just as they reached the middle of the Red Sea, the last Israelites were reaching the far shore. The waters filled up again, pouring over the Egyptians.

Activity

a) Why did Moses go to the King of Egypt?
b) Were the Israelites treated well in Egypt?
c) What type of a man was Moses?
d) Describe some of the plagues.
e) What persuaded Pharaoh to let the Israelites go free?
f) Describe how the Israelites got across the Red Sea.
g) Why couldn't the Egyptians follow them?

David and Goliath
By a soldier in King Saul's army

What should we do? Our army had been fighting the Philistines for months, but we never seemed to be winning. Every time we attacked them, they fought back and gained ground. It seemed as though we were never going to beat them.

"It's that champion of theirs," said Benjamin. "He's just too powerful!" "He's not just too powerful," chipped in Gad. "He's too big!" We laughed, but Gad was right. Goliath was big – a giant of a man. He towered over our soldiers, swinging his sword from left to right, and we stood no chance.

Suddenly, Tobiah ran past our group. "Quickly!" he shouted excitedly. "Get down to the plain. Someone else is going to fight Goliath!"

"Who is it?" We asked, jumping up and following him. Tobiah couldn't hide the laughter in his voice as he replied: "David!"
We looked at each other in disbelief. David! But he was only a boy – a shepherd boy, at that! He'd been invited to the court of King Saul as a musician. Everyone liked him but he was no soldier.

When we reached the hillside overlooking the plain, there he was. And what a ridiculous sight he made! He was wearing great heavy armour, a helmet and breastplate. He was sagging beneath the weight of a shield and sword. We stopped laughing and felt really disappointed. There was no way that this boy could beat the Philistines' giant!

"Please," I heard him say to one of the soldiers. "Take this off me. I don't need this armour. I'm not used to it"

"But it's the king's own armour. And besides, you're going to fight Goliath!" the soldier replied. David ignored him and struggled to free himself from the breastplate, until he stood in only his tunic. He looked so small and fragile. Then I noticed someone behind him: King Saul himself.

"So how will you fight, David, without weapons or armour?" he said to the boy.

"**I have God**, your majesty," he answered. "**He will protect me**. He will be my shield and my sword. As long as God is on our side, no one can harm us." Saul smiled faintly and put his hand on David's shoulder.
"Then may God be with you," he said.
"He is," David told him. "With me, with you, and with the people of Israel – *His* people!"

Then the shepherd boy turned and strode into the middle of the plain calling Goliath's name.

The Philistine army started to cheer as the earth shook and their champion appeared. It seemed so unfair that the boy would be killed; I wanted to turn away, it was almost too awful to watch. But I stayed and saw him pull something from his belt: a sling – a sort of catapult. Then, he bent down and started to pick up pebbles from the rocky ground. What on earth was he doing?

The Israelite army – my army – fell silent, watching David. But the Philistines roared with laughter. As if it hadn't been enough for us to send a boy out to fight their champion, now it looked like he was playing stones on the valley floor! "What do you think I am? A dog? You're just a boy with sticks!" he bellowed. But David stared into his eyes, no fear on his face, only a look of determination. Then his young voice echoed over the plain:

"I stand before you in the name of the Lord, the God of the Israelites' army. Today, He will make me strong, and hand you over to us. I will strike you down, Goliath. And everyone here will know that the Lord is stronger than any sword; the battle will be won by Him!"

All eyes were on David as he placed one of the pebbles in his sling and swung it faster and faster over his head. Then, with one great final swing, he threw the stone in the direction of the giant's face. The armies gasped as it flew through the air with a high pitched whistling sound, and struck Goliath right between the eyes: "Whack!" For a moment, everything was still and quiet. No one moved. Even Goliath himself remained still, his sword held high above his head. Next moment, he started to sway. He crumpled to his knees and then keeled over. The ground shook as he fell: dead.

Suddenly, an enormous cheer went up from the Israelites. We surged around David. Then, we lifted him onto our shoulders and carried him back to the camp, singing.

"The Lord God guards and protects us: great is the Lord!
He saves his people, Israel, and overcomes our enemies.
The Lord is our fortress and our strength, our shield and our sword.
Blessed be David who trusted God and defeated the giant!"

Activity

a) How was David going to fight the giant?
b) What did the people think would happen to David?
c) Who do you think helped David to win the battle?
d) What effect do you think David's victory had on the Philistines?
e) What can we learn from this account of David?

4.2 Trust in God

Religious Education Curriculum Directory
The Christmas mystery
Jesus was born in a humble stable, into a poor family. Simple shepherds were the first witnesses to this event. In this poverty, heaven's glory was made manifest. The Church never tires of singing the glory of this night:

> The Virgin today brings into the world the Eternal
> and the earth offers a cave to the Inaccessible.
> The angels and shepherds praise him
> and the magi advance with the star,
> for you are born for us,
> little Child, God eternal! (CCC 525).

Attainment Target 1: Learning *about* the Catholic faith.
Attainment Target 2: Learning *from* the Catholic faith.

Key Learning Objectives

* Understand the importance of trusting in God.
  ○ Be aware that it is not always easy for us to trust.

* Know about God's promise to Zechariah.
  ○ Reflect on how Zechariah had to trust in God.

* Know that Mary trusted in God.
  ○ Reflect on what we can learn from Mary.

* Know how Joseph put his trust in God.
  ○ Be aware that sometimes we need help to trust in God.

* Know that God fulfilled His promise to Mary when Jesus was born.
  ○ Reflect on the importance of the birth of Jesus for us.

* Know why God sent Jesus to earth.
  ○ Reflect on who Jesus is for us.

Theological Notes

Mary, Mother of God
Q. What does the Church teach about Mary?
"The Annunciation to Mary inaugurates 'the fullness of time', the time of the fulfilment of God's promises and preparations. Mary was invited to conceive him in whom the 'whole fullness of divinity' would dwell 'bodily'. The divine response to her question, 'How can this be, since I know not man?' was given by the power of the Spirit: 'The Holy Spirit will come upon you' (CCC 484).

"Mary is truly 'Mother of God' since she is the mother of the eternal Son of God made man, who is God himself" (CCC 509).

Mary's virginity

"The Gospel accounts understand the virginal conception of Jesus as a divine work that surpasses all human understanding and possibility: 'That which is conceived in her is of the Holy Spirit', said the angel to Joseph about Mary his fiancée. The Church sees here the fulfilment of the divine promise given through the prophet Isaiah: 'Behold, a virgin shall conceive and bear a son" (CCC 497).

Q. How did the Word become flesh?
"With the **Nicene Creed**, we answer by confessing: *'For us men and for our salvation* he came down from heaven; by the power of the Holy Spirit, he became incarnate of the Virgin Mary, and was made man'" (CCC 456).

Q. Why did the Word become flesh?
"The Word became flesh for us *in order to save us by reconciling us with God,* who 'loved us and sent His Son to be the expiation for our sins': 'the Father has sent his Son as the Saviour of the world', and 'he was revealed to take away sins'" (CCC 457).

"The Word became flesh *so that thus we might know God's love:* 'In this the love of God was made manifest among us, that God sent his only Son into the world, so that we might live through him.' 'For God so loved the world that He gave His only Son, that whoever believes in him should not perish but have eternal life'" (CCC 458 – see also CCC 459 & 460).

The Trinity
Q. What does the Catechism say, in brief, about the mystery of the Trinity?
"The mystery of the Most Holy Trinity is the central mystery of the Christian faith and of Christian life. God alone can make it known to us by revealing himself as Father, Son, and Holy Spirit" (CCC 261).

"The Incarnation of God's Son reveals that God is the eternal Father and that the Son is consubstantial with the Father, which means that, in the Father and with the Father, the Son is one and the same God" (CCC 262).

"The mission of the Holy Spirit, sent by the Father in the name of the Son (Jn. 14:26) and by the Son 'from the Father' (Jn. 15:26), reveals that, with them, the Spirit is one and the same God. 'With the Father and the Son he is worshipped and glorified' (Nicene Creed)" (CCC 263).

"Inseparable in what they are, the divine persons are also inseparable in what they do. But within the single, divine operation each shows forth what is proper to him in the Trinity, especially in the divine mission of the Son's Incarnation and the gift of the Holy Spirit" (CCC 267).

The Incarnation

Q. What is meant by the mystery of the Incarnation?

The word INCARNATION means that God, who is divine, took on human flesh and blood and became a real man. This is a mystery which we cannot fully understand but believe by faith. Jesus is not part God and part man; he is not a confused mixture of the divine and the human.

The **Catechism of the Catholic Church (CCC) states:**

"At the time appointed by God, the only Son of the Father, the eternal Word, that is, the Word and substantial Image of the Father, became incarnate; without losing his divine nature he has assumed human nature" (CCC 479).

"Jesus Christ is true God and true man, in the unity of his divine person; for this reason he is the one and only mediator between God and man" (CCC 480).

"Jesus Christ possesses two natures, one divine and the other human, not confused, but united in the one person of God's Son" (CCC 481).

God reveals Himself to us through Jesus, who is truly God and, as man truly human. Through Jesus, we can go directly to God and he leads us into a loving relationship with his Father.

Q. What is the importance of the *Epiphany*?

The *Epiphany* is the manifestation of Jesus as Messiah of Israel, Son of God and Saviour of the world. The great feast of Epiphany celebrates the adoration of Jesus by the wise men *(magi)* from the East, together with his baptism in the Jordan and the wedding feast at Cana in Galilee. In the magi, representatives of the neighbouring pagan religions, the Gospel sees the first-fruits of the nations, who welcome the good news of salvation through the Incarnation. The magi's coming to Jerusalem in order to pay homage to the king of the Jews shows that they seek in Israel, in the messianic light of the star of David, the one who will be king of the nations" (CCC 528).

Additional Theological Notes

Elizabeth

Background notes on Elizabeth

In Elizabeth's day, it was considered a humiliation if a married woman did not have children. She was to be pitied by some and talked about by others. Elizabeth waited, dreaming, hoping and trusting in God. As we have seen in the life of Abraham's wife, Sarah, God's ways are mysterious: prayers are answered but not in the way and time expected.

Like Sarah, it was only when Elizabeth was old and well past child bearing age that God intervened. Her cousin, Mary, came to hear her good news and to share her own. They recognise each other as being filled with God's grace and their unborn children joined in. (cf. Lk. 41-44)

Mary

Mary's role in the Annunciation and Incarnation

From the very first moment Mary appears in the New Testament, in the mystery of the Annunciation (Lk. 1:26 ff), she is set forth as the 'model of faith'. It is God who breaks into Mary's life: Mary does not go to God; it is God who comes to Mary, taking the initiative of His saving and redeeming love. Addressed by the archangel Gabriel, in God's name, as "full of grace" or "highly favoured one", Mary is "greatly troubled": there must be some mistake here; she knows herself to be the simple, humble maidservant of the Lord. "Do not be afraid, Mary," she is reassured, as were Moses and the prophets of old, or later the apostles of the new dispensation; "it is **you** who have found favour with the Lord". And when she is further told that she "will conceive and bear a son who will be called the Son of the Most High", she does not jump to appropriate this role, which every young woman in Israel was longing for – to be the mother of the Messiah. In all truth and honesty, Mary seeks to clarify her real situation: "How can this be (that I have a son), since I have no relations with men?" Once again, she is reassured, in God's name, that God and God alone will do it all: "The Holy Spirit will come upon you, and the power of the Most High will overshadow you; therefore, the child that will be born of you will be called Son of God." Even **then**, Mary does not respond, as it were appropriating the gift of the Lord; she does **not** say anything like: "All right, then, I will be the Mother of the Incarnate Lord." Her only response is that of genuine faith, that of total availability to God as God, to God's call and vocation, from her real situation and accepting herself for who she is: "I am the maidservant of the Lord; let it be done to me – not **I** shall do it – according to your Word". With all the power and energy of her free will, **Mary let God be God** in her life; Mary gave God a real, serious chance in her life.

Again, in Mary's case – as in Abraham's – this initial attitude of the response of authentic faith to God's call of love is not merely the starting-point of her mystery. It is, in fact, the whole and entire mystery of Mary, lived out progressively and in ever deepening fashion along the journey of her life and its real challenges, right up to the foot of the Cross.

Fr. Herbert Alphonso SJ

4.2 Trust in God

> Understand the importance of trusting in God.
> Be aware that it is not always easy for us to trust.

Learning to Trust

 Starting point:
The text in Pupil's Book 'Learning to Trust' could be used as a starting point. Pupils could be invited to share their experience of learning to swim or ride a bicycle.

 WS: Story of Tom and Abigail (TB p. 36)

Explain: It is important for children to understand that when we trust in God our prayers are not always answered in the way we ask, but God has other things waiting for us. God has a wonderful purpose for whatever happens. It may take years before we will understand His plan.

Guardian Angels: explain to children that we have a guardian angel. Simplify the following quotations.

"The whole life of the Church benefits from the mysterious and powerful help of angels" (CCC 334).

"From infancy to death human life is surrounded by their watchful care and intercession. Beside each believer stands an angel as protector and shepherd leading him (her) to life. Already here on earth the Christian life shares by faith in the blessed company of angels and men united in God" (CCC 336).

[Pupils will learn more from the teacher's example than from words of advice. We cannot teach children to have great faith in God if we don't show great faith in Him in all circumstances.]

 Prayer to our Guardian Angel
Angel of God, my Guardian dear, to whom God's love commits me here;
Ever this day, be at my side to light and guard; to rule and guide. Amen

 SMART page: Trust in God – Words to help us (CD ROM)

Guided Meditation: Trusting in God (CD ROM)

 Plenary - SMART page: Trusting - Key Points (CD ROM & PB p. 26)

Zechariah

Know about God's promise to Zechariah.
Reflect on how Zechariah had to trust in God.

God's promise to Zechariah

Starting point:
Invite pupils to think of something that took them completely by surprise and invite two or three to share. Explain what it was like for Zechariah. He enters the Temple and goes into the sacred space, while the people wait outside and pray. It is the hour of the evening sacrifice when he places incense on the burning coals. The fragrance of the incense rising from the thurible (censer) is a symbol of prayer.

SMART notebook: 'Zechariah' as alternative to activity 2 on page 29.

Discuss
- What does it mean to trust?
- Did Zechariah have any good reasons for trusting?
- How would you have responded if you were in his situation?
- We all like to have people we can trust, but how do we know if others feel they can trust us? Can others depend on us to do what we say?
- If we pray for something and we don't get it, what does that mean?
  (This question is to see if pupils have understood and remembered the points made in the previous lesson. Explain again that God knows what is best for us – even though we believe what we want at this particular time is best for us – God sees into the future and He will give us whatever it is that is going to make us a better person.)

Additional activities
1. It is sometimes difficult for us to keep our promises.
   a) Describe a time when you or someone you know made a difficult promise and kept it.
   b) Write what made the promise difficult to keep.
   c) Why do you think it is important to keep promises?

2. Sometimes it is hard for us to trust that God knows what is best for us.
   Write about a time when you found it hard to trust in God.
   Explain why it was difficult.

3. The angel brought a promise about John.
   a) Look up Luke 1:14-15.
   b) What was the promise?

Plenary: What can we learn from Zechariah's experience?

Mary trusts in God

Know that Mary trusted in God.
Reflect on what we can learn from Mary.

The Annunciation

Notes for Teacher: *When the angel tells Mary that she has been chosen to be the mother of the Messiah, she replies, "How shall this be, since I have no husband?" (Lk. 1:34). Mary was betrothed, which meant that according to Jewish law, she was already a married woman, even if she did not yet live with her husband and they had not yet begun their conjugal life. The angel confirms that her motherhood will not come about in the normal way after she had been taken home by Joseph, but through "overshadowing, by the power of the Most High," by the coming of the Holy Spirit … for with God nothing is impossible" (Lk. 1:37).*

 Starting point:
Explain that we are now going to think about the angel Gabriel appearing to Mary to tell her that God had chosen her to be the mother of His son.

Mary was humble, poor and unknown. Her heart was open and ready to do God's will. She was willing to let God work through her.

Draw pupils' attention to the picture in the PB p. 30.

How can we be like Mary? (*The best way is to make time to pray to Jesus each day and ask Mary to help us to stay close to him.*)

 Additional activities
1. a) Look at the list of things Mary had to trust God to do when she said 'yes' to Him.

   Mary had to trust God:
   - to help Joseph to understand that her baby was the Son of God;
   - to let the baby be born safely in the place God chose;
   - to protect her and the baby from all danger.

   b) Choose one of the above bullet points and explain why Mary might have been anxious.

2. **WS:** Mary visits Elizabeth (TB p. 37 & CD ROM)

3. **WS:** Mary's Song of Praise (CD ROM)

 PPP: Advent

 Prayer
God our Father,
Mary our Mother was always ready to do whatever you asked of her.
Help us to be more like Mary so that we are ready to listen to your voice.
Help us to be willing to do what you ask of us.
Give us the help we need to show kindness to those we meet.

Joseph trusts in God

Know how Joseph put his trust in God.
Be aware that sometimes we need help to trust in God.

Joseph puts his trust in God

Notes for Teacher: Mary was betrothed to Joseph. So Mary could be called Joseph's wife even though he had not yet taken her to his home – the step which would have classified them as married. According to the Jewish law, while betrothed the woman still lived with her parents. After a year her husband would have taken her to his own home which would have sealed their marriage. Now Joseph has to face the fact that Mary "was with child of the Holy Spirit" (Matt. 1:18).

Joseph has to assume that Mary has broken their engagement and according to Jewish law he must dismiss her. He can bring Mary before the court or he can issue her with a private writ of divorce. He decides to do it privately in order "not to put her to shame" (Matt. 1:10). This shows that Joseph was a just man. (Cf. Pope Benedict XVI, Jesus of Nazareth Infancy Narratives 2012)

Starting point
Explain that we can assume that Joseph must have been praying earnestly to God for guidance because when the angel Gabriel appeared to him in a dream, he knew immediately that it was God's messenger that had truly spoken to him. When he woke from sleep, he took Mary home to be his wife.
- Recap on the ways Mary had to trust in God.
- In what ways did Joseph have to trust in God?

Note: Activity 1 PB p. 33 *There were no mobile phones or email for Mary and Joseph to make a booking – however, they **trusted completely in God alone.***

SMART notebook: **Joseph** – which of the words best describe him? Give reasons for your answer. (Alternative to activity 3 in PB p. 33)

Additional activity
WS: Make a 'coat-hanger' poem about St. Joseph. (CD ROM)
(It is called a coat-hanger poem because you can put words on each side of the letters.)

Discuss: The angel of the Lord told Joseph to call the baby 'Jesus' because "he will save his people from their sins" (Matt. 1:21-22). Like all Jews Mary and Joseph would have known that only God can forgive sins.
   a) What questions do you think Mary and Joseph might have asked each other about the words of the angel?
   b) What answers do you think they might have given to each other?

Plenary: What do you admire most about St. Joseph? Why?

God fulfils His Promise

Know that God fulfilled His promise to Mary when Jesus was born.
Reflect on the importance of the birth of Jesus for us.

 Starting point
Imagine the journey Mary and Joseph had to make to Bethlehem.
They knew that their baby would be very special.
- What kind of a place do you think they would like to have for him?
- In what kind of a place do you think a great king would be born?

Now read what happened in the PB pp. 34-35.

 Additional activities
1. a) Think about the account of the birth of Jesus.
   Choose a character, a time, a place and the weather.
   b) Now write your account of what happened using the character you have chosen.
   c) Why is the birth of Jesus important for us today?

2. a) What was the news that the angel brought to the shepherds?
   b) How would they know it was true? (Clue – Luke 2:2-12)

 PPP: Visit of the Wise Men (CD ROM)

 SMART notebook: **How to be like Mary** (CD ROM)

Pause to reflect: The True Meaning of Christmas
- Who is this baby? *(God in human form)*
- Where is he born? *(In a stable)*
- Who welcomes him? *(The shepherds who were minding their sheep and the wise men who followed the star).*

 PPP: Flight into Egypt (CD ROM)

 SMART notebook: **What does the birth of Jesus mean for us?**

WS: Christmas Cards (CD ROM).

 On a 'post it note' pupils write down two ways they can help their family to remember the true meaning of Christmas. The teacher can share them with the class if there is time or at the start of the next lesson.

 SMART notebook: Glossary

Mysteries of our Faith

Know why God sent Jesus to earth.
Reflect on who Jesus is for us.

Mystery of the Trinity

Note for Teachers: In order to help pupils become religiously literate, that is, to have a sound religious and theological framework of knowledge appropriate to their age, it is necessary to help them understand the basics of religion and theology and how they link to their lives and experience. For this reason, it is essential to build on the hierarchy of Truths in the teaching of the Church, that is, that some Truths depend on others for their validity. For example, pupils need to have some knowledge of the Trinity in order to grasp that in Jesus, God comes to earth and that he is truly and fully God and fully human.

Starting point

What is the first thing we usually do when we are going to pray? (Make the sign of the Cross). Think deeply - what does it mean to make the Sign of the Cross? (We profess the deepest mysteries of our Christian Faith – the Trinity: Father, Son and Holy Spirit and how Jesus has saved us from sin and death by dying on the Cross for us.)

Explain that in this lesson we are going to explore what the Trinity means and why it is important. The Trinity is a wonderful mystery. Although we can never fully understand it, our human minds are designed to think about it, to reflect on it and work out what we can say about it.

Prayers to the Trinity

Sign of the Cross: In the name of the Father and of the Son and of the Holy Spirit. Amen.

Glory be to the Father and to the Son and to the Holy Spirit, as it was in the beginning, is now and ever shall be, world without end. Amen.

PPP: The Trinity (CD ROM)
PPP: Mystery of the Incarnation (CD ROM)

Plenary: What does the birth of Jesus mean for us?

(Test knowledge of the key points; if necessary use the SMART notebook again for recall).

- Jesus, truly God and truly human, has come down to earth.
- He brings peace, love and true freedom to those who seek him.
- If you truly seek Jesus, he will find you.
- It is not money or knowledge that matters, Jesus seeks those looking for him.
- Jesus has come for all of us.

Tom and Abigail

Tom learns to trust

Sometimes it can be very hard to trust, to really be sure that everything is going to be all right. Read what happened to Tom.

It had been raining hard for hours, and the children were getting bored watching TV. "What's that noise outside?" Abigail asked, and they all rushed to the window.

Instead of the road and the pavement, there was a rushing river of water! Just then the front door burst open and the water poured in. The children raced upstairs. Rebecca ran to the window.

"There's a boat coming down the street!" she shouted. "It's the lifeboat; it's coming to rescue us!"

There were already several people in the lifeboat. "Jump in!" shouted one of the men. "We'll catch you." Rebecca climbed on the windowsill and took a deep breath. She shut her eyes and jumped, landing safely in the boat. Then Abigail jumped as well. Now it was Tom's turn. He scrambled onto the windowsill and looked down. The boat was even more crowded now. He couldn't see where he would land if he jumped. He felt his legs begin to shake.

"I don't think I can do this," he called. "I feel a bit wobbly. I'm afraid the boat will sink." "Come on, lad," shouted one of the crew, "We'll catch you."

"Don't be afraid, Tom," called Abigail. "You'll be quite safe. We jumped and we're safe inside the boat now. The boat is made to carry a lot more people than this. It won't sink – you can trust it." Tom still felt very shaky, but he knew he had to trust. "OK," he said in a small voice, shut his eyes, and jumped.

Strong arms reached out to catch him – he had made it! Now that he was inside the boat he could see how big it was and how safe. It was difficult to trust, but I'm glad I did, he thought, and watched as the boat pulled away from the flooded house, taking them all to safety.

Mary visits Elizabeth

"Mary set out at that time and went as quickly as she could to a town in the hill country of Judah. She went into Zechariah's house and greeted Elizabeth.

Now as soon as Elizabeth heard Mary's greeting, the child leapt in her womb and Elizabeth was filled with the Holy Spirit. She gave a loud cry and said, 'Of all women you are the most blessed, and blessed is the fruit of your womb. Why should I be honoured with a visit from the mother of my Lord? For the moment your greeting reached my ears, the child in my womb leapt for joy. Yes, blessed is she who believed that the promise made her by the Lord would be fulfilled'" (Lk. 1:39-45).

Mary is blessed because she believed the Word of God.

Activities

1. Read: Mary's Song of Praise, (Lk. 1:46-48).
   Imagine you overhear Mary and Elizabeth. Who said the following?
   a) "My baby jumped for joy when you came in!"
   b) "I am so happy – I will sing a song of praise to God."
   c) "I never thought that the Mother of God's Son would come to visit me."
   d) "People will call me blessed now."

2. Use the words above and some more of your own to make a short play script of the meeting between Elizabeth and Mary.

4.3 Jesus, the Teacher

Religious Education Curriculum Directory

Catechism of the Catholic Church

"The Gospels are the heart of all the Scriptures because they are our principal source for the life and teaching of the Incarnate Word, our Saviour" (CCC 125).

"The Beatitudes respond to the natural desire for happiness. This desire is of divine origin: God has placed it in the human heart in order to draw man to the One who alone can fulfil it" (CCC 1718).

Attainment Target 1: Learning *about* the Catholic faith.
Attainment Target 2: Learning *from* the Catholic faith.

Key Learning Objectives

- Know that Mary and Joseph took Jesus to the Temple.
  - Reflect on what this means for us.

- Know that Jesus was born a Jew.
  - Reflect on how Mary and Joseph found Jesus in the Temple.

- Know about the Baptism of Jesus.
  - Reflect on what Jesus' baptism means for us.

- Know that Jesus called people to follow him.
  - Be aware that we are also called to follow Jesus.

- Know that Jesus travelled around teaching people.
  - Think about the Good News that Jesus teaches.

- Know some of the parables Jesus used to teach people.
  - Reflect on the meaning of the parables for us.

- Know that Jesus came to show us the way to live. (The Beatitudes)
  - Think of ways in which we can be true followers of Jesus.
    (Text in TB and CD ROM only)

Theological Notes

Q. What is the significance of the Presentation of Jesus in the Temple?

"The presentation of Jesus in the temple shows him to be the firstborn Son who belongs to the Lord. With Simeon and Anna, all Israel awaits its *encounter* with the Saviour – the name given to this event in the Byzantine tradition. Jesus is recognised as the long-expected Messiah, the 'light to the nations' and the 'glory of Israel', but also a 'sign that is spoken against'.

The sword of sorrow predicted for Mary announces Christ's perfect and unique oblation on the cross that will impart the salvation God has 'prepared in the presence of all people'" (CCC 529).

In this 'external' observance, both Jesus and Mary were 'interiorly' (in their hearts) repeating and deepening their self-offering and self-gift to God the Father's holy will (**Jesus** - Hebrews 10:5-10; **Mary** - Luke 1:28).

Simeon and Anna (Luke 2:22-38) had 'open hearts'; they were led by the Spirit of God and recognised in Jesus the Saviour of the world (the 'light of the world').

Q. What do we know about the early life of Jesus?
"During the greater part of his life, Jesus shared the condition of the vast majority of human beings: a daily life spent without evident greatness, a life of manual labour. His religious life was that of a Jew obedient to the law of God, a life in the community" (CCC 531).

Q. What is important about the 'Finding of Jesus in the Temple'?
"The finding of Jesus in the temple is the only event that breaks the silence of the Gospels about the hidden years of Jesus. Here Jesus lets us catch a glimpse of the mystery of his total consecration to a mission that flows from his divine sonship: 'Did you not know that I must be about my Father's work?' Mary and Joseph did not understand these words, but they accepted them in faith. Mary 'kept all these things in her heart' during the years Jesus remained hidden in the silence of an ordinary life" (CCC 534).

Q. What is important about the 'Baptism of Jesus'?
"Jesus' public life begins with his baptism by John in the Jordan. John preaches 'a baptism of repentance for the forgiveness of sins'. A crowd of sinners – tax collectors and soldiers, Pharisees and Sadducees, and prostitutes come to be baptised by him. 'Then Jesus appears.' The Baptist hesitates, but Jesus insists and receives baptism. Then the Holy Spirit, in the form of a dove, comes upon Jesus and a voice from heaven proclaims, 'This is my beloved Son.' This is the manifestation (Epiphany) of Jesus as Messiah of Israel and Son of God" (CCC 535).

In his baptism "the Spirit whom Jesus possessed in fullness from his conception comes to 'rest on him'. Jesus will be the source of the Spirit for all mankind. At his baptism 'the heavens were opened' – the heavens that Adam's sin had closed – and the waters were sanctified by the descent of Jesus and the Spirit, a prelude to the new creation" (CCC 536).

Q. What are the Beatitudes?
"The Beatitudes reveal the goal of human existence, the ultimate end of human acts: God calls us to His own beatitude. This vocation is addressed to each individual personally, but also to the Church as a whole, the new people made up of those who have accepted the promise and live from it in faith" (CCC 1719).

"God put us in the world to know, to love and to serve Him and so to come to paradise. Beatitude makes us 'partakers of the divine nature' and of eternal life. With beatitude, man enters into the glory of Christ and into the joy of the Trinitarian life" (CCC 1721).

Q. Why does Jesus teach in parables?
"Jesus' invitation to enter his kingdom comes in the form of *parables*, a characteristic feature of his teaching. Through his parables he invites people to the feast of the kingdom, but he also asks for a radical choice: to gain the kingdom, one must give everything. Words are not enough, deeds are required. The parables are like mirrors for man: will he be hard soil or good earth for the word? What use will he make of the talents he has received? Jesus and the presence of the kingdom in this world are secretly at the heart of the parables. One must enter the kingdom, that is, become a disciple of Christ, in order to 'know the secrets of the kingdom of heaven.' For those who stay 'outside', everything remains enigmatic" (CCC 546).

ADDITIONAL THEOLOGICAL NOTES

Q. What is the significance of the 'Presentation of the Child Jesus in the Temple'?
Mary and Joseph take Jesus to be presented in the Temple, forty days after his birth, according to the Law. Concentrating on the person and mystery of Mary, we note that Mary is not just fulfilling the Mosaic Law. She is making the gift of herself with her Son, making the total gift of herself in active availability to God, His Word and His call for her. It is in this scene that the holy old man Simeon speaks to Mary and Joseph after they have presented the child Jesus. Taking the child in his arms, Simeon blesses God and, in chanting his hymn, the *Nunc Dimittis*, acknowledges that God has revealed to him the Saving One, the Messiah, in the child he is holding in his arms.

Simeon then turns to Mary; in his words to her, we are given a revelation central to the mystery of Mary: "This child is a sign of contradiction, set for the fall and the rise of many in Israel; and a sword will pierce your own soul, your own heart, that the thoughts of many hearts may be revealed" (Lk. 2:34-35). What 'sword'? The Word of God is the 'sword': it is Jesus who is the 'sword'. Mary is representative of the 'People of God'; it is in the 'sword' piercing and penetrating her soul or heart that the people are shown up, either as individual persons or groups of persons, for who they really are: true or false disciples of Jesus Christ: Mary becomes, in this sense, an authentic disciple of Jesus Christ. Those who, like Mary, are open and available to the Word of God will be recognised as Jesus' authentic disciples; those who are not actively available to God's Word will be discerned to be false and spurious disciples.

Q. What is most important about the loss and finding of Jesus in the Temple?
"When Jesus was twelve years old (and we know that in the Jewish law, a Jewish boy

becomes an adult at the age of thirteen, becoming as he does bar-mitzvah, son of the law), he was lost in the temple, and his mother and foster father found him there after looking for him over three days of great anguish and sorrow. We recall that his mother said to him: "Why have you done such a thing to us? We have been looking for you with hearts full of sorrow and anxiety." What was Jesus' response? With calm intransigence he replied: "How is it you looked for me? Did you not know that I must be about my Father's business? Did you not know that I must be in the house of my Father and the things that concern my Father?" Already at the age of twelve, his life-orientation was clear. His identity was clear; he lived **only** for his Father. He was inviting his mother and foster-father to this freedom for the Father **alone."**

Q. What is most important about the call of the first disciples?

One day Jesus was preaching the Word of God on the shores of the Lake of Galilee. The crowds were pressing in on him. He noticed two boats moored to the shore, the fishermen had left them to go and wash their nets. Getting into Simon Peter's boat, he asked him to move a little way into the water so that he could speak to the crowd. When he had finished speaking, Jesus said to Peter: "Launch out into the deep, and let down your nets for a catch". Peter reacted in all sincerity: "Master, we have toiled and laboured all night, and have caught nothing!" But he added immediately: "But, Master, at **your** Word I shall let down the nets." He did so, and there was such a huge catch of fish that the nets were at breaking-point – so much so, that Peter had to cry out for help from his companions in the other boat. At a few words from the Master, Peter witnessed that the two boats were filled with an immense haul of fish and were about to sink. He fell down at the feet of Jesus and cried out: "Depart from me, for I am a sinful man, O Lord!"

Peter recognised in Jesus the holy one of God, and openly acknowledged his own sinfulness before the holiness of this Master and Lord. This same Lord and Master now lifted him up and said: "Do not be afraid, Peter; from now on, you will be catching not fish, but people". "And when they (Peter and his companions) had brought their boats to land, they left everything (boats, nets and all) and followed him" (Lk. 5:1-11).

St. Mark's account of the call of the Twelve Apostles

"Jesus went up to the hills, and called to him those whom he desired; and they came to him. And he appointed twelve, to be with him, and to be sent out to preach and have authority to cast out demons: Simon whom he surnamed Peter; James, the son of Zebedee and John, the brother of James, whom he surnamed Boanerges, that is, sons of thunder; then Andrew, Philip, Bartholomew, Matthew, Thomas, James the son of Alphaeus, Thaddaeus, Simon the Zealot and Judas Iscariot, who betrayed him" (Mk. 3:13-19).

Reflection on the call of the Twelve Apostles

Notice that the entire passage, from start to finish, turns around one single pronoun *'he'*. "**He** went up into the hills, and called to **him** those whom **he** desired; and they came **to him**. And **he** appointed twelve to be **with him**, and to be sent out to preach and have authority to cast out demons" (vv. 13-15). Now this is not a chance repetition of the personal pronoun 'he' – that is, **Jesus**. I strongly believe that the Word of God is communicating to us that *he* (**the Person of Jesus** is the deepest meaning of the apostolic call, activity and ministry. Note that those called to be *active apostles,* to be **with him** and (only in virtue of being **with him**) are to be sent out to preach.

These twelve men were very different persons, each of them with his own peculiar temperament and character, his own strengths and weaknesses. Simon Peter always comes through as 'impetuous', ever ready to walk two steps ahead of the Lord; James and John, Zebedee's sons, called 'sons of thunder', accurately expressing their fiery zeal and somewhat vaulting ambition; Andrew and Philip, who constantly come across as utterly simple persons; the cynical Bartholomew or Nathanael who could only respond, "Can anything good come out of Nazareth?", when told by Philip that they had found Jesus of Nazareth whom Moses and the prophets wrote; Matthew the tax-collector, perhaps the only learned one among all the twelve; and, of course, the 'doubting' Thomas who refused to believe that the rest of the apostles had, in his absence, seen and talked to the Risen Jesus, until he himself had the chance of seeing in Jesus' hands the print of the nails and of placing his finger in Jesus' wounds and his hand in Jesus' pierced side.

All of the apostles were very different men, but all had one feature in common: *"he"* personally called each and all of them, to be **"with him"** and, only so, to receive his own personal mission of the ministry of the Word and the ministry of liberation in the power of the Word. Of the last named apostle, Judas, it is not said that he committed this or that heinous crime: all the horror of his sin is captured most eloquently in what he did to **the Person of Jesus** – Judas "betrayed *him*"! The entire passage that began with **"he"**, then continued with **"to him"** and **"with him"**, closes with this final note: "Judas Iscariot, who betrayed **him**".

Fr. Herbert Alphonso SJ

4.3 Jesus, the Teacher

> **Know that Mary and Joseph took Jesus to the Temple.**
> **Reflect on what this means for us.**

The Presentation of Jesus in the Temple

 Starting point

Explain that Mary and Joseph were faithful Jews and Jesus was born a Jew. It was a rule among the Jews that the first boy child born to a family was to be taken to the Temple in Jerusalem. Mary and Joseph took Jesus and handed him over personally to God. From now on Jesus belongs completely to God.

 Read: Jesus is presented in the Temple (Lk. 2:22-32) to the pupils to reflect on before using the Pupil's Book.

Additional activity

Imagine you are a newspaper reporter and you were there in the Temple when Mary and Joseph brought in the child Jesus.

  a) Think of a headline for a report of what you saw and heard.
  b) Write the headline in large capital letters.
  c) Underneath, write a short report of the event. Explain what happened and why.

Explain that the Feast of the 'Presentation of Jesus in the Temple' is on 2nd February each year. Sometimes there is a procession with lighted candles at Mass on this day, so it is also called 'Candlemas'. The significance of the lighted candles is that Jesus is the 'light' that has come into the world.

Discuss:

* Why do you think Simeon was so happy to see the infant Jesus?
* How did he know who Jesus was? *(Because Simeon is a holy man; he had been praying for the coming of the Redeemer, the Saviour. He is a man of hope and expectation; in a way he already has the Holy Spirit upon him. He is tuned in to the presence of God so he speaks like a prophet. He takes the child, praises God, saying "At last, all-powerful Master, you give leave to your servant to go in peace … for my eyes have seen your salvation … (Lk. 2:29-32).*
* What do you think Simeon meant by saying "my eyes have seen your salvation"? *(He recognised that Jesus is the Saviour who brings salvation).*
* Who is the Messiah? *(Explain that Messiah is another name for 'saviour' and that Jesus had come to save all people).*
* How did Anna know who Jesus was? *(Because she spent all her time with God and for God. She was filled with His Spirit.)*

 Note: *The Prayer of Simeon, the Nunc Dimittis, is used every evening in the Divine Office - Prayer of the Church, Compline.*

 Plenary: What were the most important points in today's lesson? Make a list.

Jesus in the Temple

Know that Jesus was born a Jew.
Reflect on how Mary and Joseph found Jesus in the Temple.

Jesus was born a Jew

Notes for Teacher *– It is essential to make clear to children that Jesus was born into a Jewish family. Mary and Joseph were faithful Jews and with Jesus, they followed the Jewish way of life. When they went to the synagogue on the Sabbath, they took Jesus with them. He was brought up with a deep love, understanding and knowledge of Jewish scriptures, history and tradition. When he was thirteen years old, he became a Bar Mitzvah which meant he was a 'Son of the Commandments'.*

The most obvious belief that Jews and Christians share is in God, the one and only God, the creator of everything, who gives and sustains life. God guides human beings and calls us into a relationship based on prayer, worship, family life and ethical living.

In what way do Jews and Christians differ?

*Jews **do not** accept that Jesus is the promised Messiah and truly God. They believe that the Messiah will come at the end of time.*

*Christians believe that Jesus is the Messiah, truly God and that he will come **again** at the end of time.*

Jews recognise Jesus as a very good teacher. While some of his ethical teachings are accepted by them, he does not play a significant part in their religion.

Starting point
What do we know about Jews?

PPP: Jewish Worship of God
(Also www.bbc.co.uk/schools/religion/judaism Beliefs; Bar Mitzvah; worship.

WS in TB page 51 **Jewish Worship of God** (CD ROM)

Explain – The Temple

There was only one Temple and it was in Jerusalem.
The Temple was the house of God where Jews believe that God was present in the Ark of the Covenant.
The Jews went to the Temple to worship God and offer sacrifices.

The Synagogue

There was a synagogue in every Jewish town.
The synagogue is a meeting place. The Jews go to the synagogue to meet together to pray, to learn the Holy Scriptures and to help each other.

The Torah

The *Torah* (Law) is the name for the first five books of the Bible. These books are also known as the Pentateuch. They are especially sacred to the Jews. Today, the *Torah* is kept in the synagogue in the form of a scroll.

What is the *Torah* all about?

The *Torah* describes events from the creation of the world to the death of Moses. It contains 613 commandments which continue to inspire and guide daily Jewish life.

Additional activities

1. Make a 'passport' for the young Jesus.
   Use the following headlines to help you:
   - Nationality
   - Parents
   - Religion
   - Place of birth
   - Place of residence

2. Why do you think the words of the **Shema** (Pupil's Book p. 42) are so important that the Jewish people repeat them every day?

3. Is there a prayer that is so important to you that you repeat it daily?
   a) What is it?
   b) Why is it important?

Loss and Finding of Jesus in the Temple

Read Luke 2: 41-45 with the class and then continue with text in Pupil's Book.

Discuss - Loss & Finding of Jesus
- Why did Mary, Joseph and Jesus go to Jerusalem?
- What happened on their way home? Why?
- What did they do? How were they feeling?
- Where did they find Jesus? What was he doing?
- What did Mary say to him? What was his reply?
- What do you think Jesus meant by his reply?

Pause to Reflect: Mary kept the words of Jesus in her heart; she did not understand, but she knew God was teaching her something. Sometimes we do not understand what happens and we have to trust God to be with us and to help us.

Plenary
Invite pupils to share the two most important points they learned today.

The Baptism of Jesus

Know about the baptism of Jesus.
Reflect on what Jesus' baptism means for us.

Zechariah's Prophecy

 Starting point

Explain that Zechariah's prophecy is a *little bit* like headline news. Look at the Pupil's Book page 44. Pupils work in pairs or small groups to discuss the meaning of the quotations and then share with the class.

Discussion points:
- What does it mean that Jesus will give light to people living in darkness? Give examples of darkness inside people? *(sadness; anger; worry; hatred; fear; loneliness)*
- How does Jesus give light? What does he say that will help people to overcome the darkness? *(He asks people to be ready to forgive those who hurt them; to love one another; to trust in him; to pray for what they need, etc.)*
- In what way does Jesus save us from our sins? *(Think of the Sacrament of Reconciliation, Pupil's Book 3 pages 49-53).*
- In what ways does Jesus make known the loving-kindness of God? *(Think of the miracles Jesus worked to heal people who were blind or crippled; the parables of the Lost Sheep; the Good Samaritan, etc. and we know he is always ready to forgive our sins when we ask him).*

The Baptism of Jesus – key points
- It reveals who Jesus really is.
- It is a public announcement that Jesus has come to fulfil God's plan.
- The dove symbolises God's Spirit coming upon Jesus.
- The dove is also a symbol of the peace that Jesus will give to all people of good will.

Study the illustration of the Baptism of Jesus, Pupil's Book page 46.
In what ways is the presence of the Trinity visible in the picture?
- *Heavens were opened – strong light shining down on Jesus and the voice spoke from heaven – the Father*
- *The dove – symbol of the Holy Spirit*
- *Jesus is present physically.*

 Additional Activities

1. Briefly describe what happened at the baptism of Jesus.

2. Explain in your own words the meaning of the baptism of Jesus.

 Plenary

Why is it important to know about the Baptism of Jesus?
In what ways does it help us to know about Jesus?

Disciples of Jesus

Know that Jesus called people to follow him.
Be aware that we are also called to follow Jesus.

Jesus chooses his first disciples

Starting point
Discuss: What type of people **do you think** Jesus wants to choose to be his close friends? Give reasons. What type do you choose? Why?

Notes for Teacher: Help the pupils to understand that Jesus chose his friends, not for what they were or could do at that time, (they were ordinary working men with little education) but for what they would do and become, and for their trust in him. All the time Jesus was with these, his friends, he loved and accepted them – each and all – just as they were. Explain that we call the friends of Jesus his disciples and that this means followers.

Why did Jesus call disciples?
Jesus had come to set up God's Kingdom. He wanted to change the whole world, to bring God's love and peace to everyone. He needed people to help him.

Read Pupil's Book - Jesus chooses his first disciples.
* What do you notice about the people he called?
* Did they ask for time to think about it?
* Was this the best thing to do? Why? Why not?
* Is there a difference between a call from Jesus and a call from a friend?

WATCH PPP: The Twelve Disciples

Additional activities
1. Why do you think Jesus chose ordinary working men rather than religious experts to follow him?

2. What would be the main differences between:
   a) being a follower of Jesus;
   b) following a famous sports or music personality?

3. Read about Jesus appointing the twelve disciples in Mark 3:13-19.
   a) Choose one of the disciples and draw two large thought bubbles.
   b) In the bubbles write some questions that may have come into this disciple's head.
   c) Underneath write the answers you think Jesus would have given.

Reflection: Song '**You have Called Us**', CD Share the Light by Bernadette **Farrell**, available from www.viewpoint24.co.uk

The Teaching of Jesus

Know that Jesus travelled around teaching people.
Think about the Good News that Jesus teaches.

Jesus' Mission

 Starting point

Explain that when Jesus started his mission he went to the synagogue. He was handed the scroll of the prophet Isaiah and read: **"The Spirit of the Lord is upon me, because He has chosen me to bring good news to the poor"** (Lk. 4:18).

All the people were amazed at the way Jesus taught, because he spoke with authority. He started to work miracles so people brought the sick, the lame and the blind to him and he cured many people. The **Good News** that Jesus brought is that **God loves us so much that he sent His Son, Jesus, to open the way to heaven for us.**

 PPP: Miracles of Jesus.

 Additional activities

1. a) Read again Matt. 25:34-37 on page 51.
   b) What is Jesus asking us to do about these people?
   c) Why is it important that we follow his teaching?

 2. **SMART notebook:** Glossary

3. Explain how the good things that you and other pupils do to help others make a difference to the lives of many people. You could present it as a flow diagram or thinking map.

4. **SMART** notebook: 'Helping Others'.

 5. **SMART** notebook: **'Our actions are like ripples in a pool'** (PB p. 52).

6. Write a list of 'good resolutions' that would help your class to be amongst the true followers of Jesus.

 Song: 'Together We'll Share' – CD More Stories & Songs of Jesus disc 2 no. 8; available from McCrimmons Publishing.

 Prayer

Lord, teach me to be generous.
Teach me to serve you as you deserve;
to give and not to count the cost,
to fight and not to heed the wounds,
to toil and not to seek for rest,
to labour and not to ask for reward,
save that of knowing that I do your will.

St. Ignatius of Loyola

The Parables

Know some of the parables Jesus used to teach people.
Reflect on the meaning of the parables for us.

Jesus used parables to teach people

Starting point
Google some images of farmers sowing seeds and some of the crops or flowers that result from the seeds.

Explain that Jesus told the parable of the Sower to dramatize the four typical ways people respond to his miracles and teaching. A farmer sowed seed in his field. (In those times, farmers sowed seed on top of the soil and ploughed it under).
PB pages 54-55.

PPP: 'The Sower'.

SMART notebook: **'The Sower'.**

Plenary: Three Questions
- What seedbed are you in?
- Why are you there?
- What might you do to get out of it?

PPP: 'The Unforgiving Servant'.

PPP: 'Evaluating Behaviour'
Invite pupils to evaluate their kindness towards their families using this scale:
0 = never, 1 = rarely, 2 = sometimes, 3 = usually, 4 = always.

a. Am I kind and helpful?
b. Do I accept correction well?
c. Do I help out without needing to be asked?
d. Do I apologise when necessary?
e. Do I pray for members of my family?

Evaluate
- 20-16   I am a joy (I hope)
- 15-10   I am OK (I think)
- 9-5   I'm not so good (Ouch!)
- 4-1   I am a problem! (Help!)

Reflect on what you could do to make sure you are a joy to your family. Write it down.

Plenary: On a 'post it' note write down what you found most helpful in the lesson. (No need to put names on it as you can use it as a 'starter' in the next lesson).

The Beatitudes

Know that Jesus came to show us the way to live.
Think of ways we can be true followers of Jesus.

Jesus shows us the way to live

Starting point
People loved to listen to Jesus teaching. One day a large crowd was following him eager to hear him. He went up a hill, so that he could see the crowd and they could see him. He sat down and taught the people about the **blessings** they will have if they follow his teaching.

WS: 'The Beatitudes' – text and activities in TB pages 52-53.

PPP: 'The Beatitudes' – interactive.

Additional Activities

1. Choose one of the Beatitudes and write a modern-day account of someone who is putting it into practice.

2. a) Study the Beatitudes. Choose two that you believe help you to live a good life. Give examples of what you do.
   b) Choose two more Beatitudes that you have seen someone else live out in his or her life. Give examples of what this person does.

3. Choose a Beatitude which you are going to 'live out' for a week. Keep a diary to record the times you did and didn't succeed.

4. In small groups act out an occasion where someone intervenes in a situation to put a Beatitude into practice.

5. Imagine you were in the crowd listening to Jesus teaching the Beatitudes. Write the conversation you had with friends on the way home about his words.

Websites: PDF The Beatitudes for children – situations and solutions
www.osv.com/Portals/0/images/pdf/BeatitudesSituations.pdf

The Beatitudes – Religious Education Programme
www.iccreligiouseducation.com/the_beatitudes.cfm

Prayer: Dear Jesus, be the beginning and end of all that we think, do and say. Prompt our actions by your grace and complete them with your all-powerful love.

Jewish Worship of God

Know what Jews believe about the Word of God

Jews believe that the Torah is the Word of God Himself, so the scrolls are kept in a special place in the synagogue, called the Ark. There is a curtain in front of the Ark and a light, which is never allowed to go out, is kept burning near it. This reminds the Jewish people that God is with them in his Word. A candleholder with seven branches called a menorah, stands in front of the Ark.

Match these words with the correct meaning and picture:

Synagogue   Rabbi   Ark   Torah   Menorah

A. The building where the Jewish people meet together to pray, to learn the Holy Scriptures and to help each other.

B. The place in the synagogue where the Word of God is carefully kept.

C. The first five books (scrolls) of the Old Testament which are especially sacred to the Jewish people.

D. A candleholder with seven branches which stands in front of the Ark.

E. Someone who teaches about God, especially in the synagogue.

The Beatitudes

Beatitudes (Lk. 6:20-23)
As usual, a large crowd was following Jesus eager to hear his teaching.

He went up a hill, so that he could see the crowd and they could see him. He sat down and taught the people about the **blessings** they will have if they follow his teaching.

"Blessed are the poor in spirit,
  for theirs is the kingdom of heaven."

The 'poor in spirit' are those who know that they need God's help every day in order to be good. So every morning we ask God to be with us and help us.

"Blessed are the meek,
  for they shall inherit the earth."

The meek are those who want to help the poor and those who are kind and thoughtful to everyone.

"Blessed are those who mourn
  for they shall be comforted."

We mourn when we have been treated unjustly. Also, we mourn when we are very sorry because we have hurt someone.

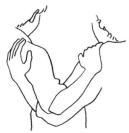

"Blessed are the merciful,
  for they shall obtain mercy."

The merciful are those willing to forgive those who hurt them.

"Blessed are those who hunger and thirst for righteousness, for they shall be satisfied."

The righteous are those who tell the truth and stand up for what is right.

"Blessed are the pure in heart, for they shall see God."

The pure in heart are those who try to make time for God in their lives.

"Blessed are those persecuted for righteousness sake, for theirs is the kingdom of heaven."

Those who are made fun of because they believe in God.

"Blessed are the peacemakers, for they shall be called the children of God."

Peacemakers are those who believe each person is precious; those who protect others from bullying.

Activities

1. The following words and phrases describe behaviour and values which go against the Beatitudes:

   bullying   selfishness   getting even   telling lies

   flattering someone to get something   looking out for yourself, not others

   Can you find a Beatitude which describes the opposite behaviour and values to those above?

2. Choose a Beatitude which you are going to 'live out' for a week. Keep a diary to record the times you did (and didn't).

4.4 Jesus, the Saviour

Religious Education Curriculum Directory
Catechism of the Catholic Church
"Jesus Christ is true God and true man, in the unity of his divine person; for this reason he is the one and only mediator between God and man" (CCC 480).

"The Paschal mystery of Christ's cross and Resurrection stands at the centre of the Good News that the apostles, and the Church following them, are to proclaim to the world. God's saving plan was accomplished 'once and for all' by the redemptive death of His Son Jesus Christ" (CCC 571).

Attainment Target 1: Learning **about** the Catholic faith.
Attainment Target 2: Learning **from** the Catholic faith.

Key Learning Objectives

- Know that Jesus is truly God and, as man, truly human.
  - Reflect on what this means for us.

- Know about Jesus' entry into Jerusalem.
  - Think about the importance of Holy Week for us.

- Understand what happened on Holy Thursday.
  - Reflect on how we can show our love for Jesus.

- Know what happened on Good Friday.
  - Reflect on the suffering of Jesus.

- Begin to understand why Jesus died on the Cross.
  - Think about what this means for us.

- Understand what happened on Easter Sunday.
  - Reflect on the importance for us of the resurrection of Jesus.

Theological Notes

Catechism Of The Catholic Church

Q. What does the Church teach about Jesus, true God and true Man?
"The unique and altogether singular event of the Incarnation of the Son of God does not mean that Jesus Christ is part God and part man, nor does it imply that he is the result of a confused mixture of the divine and the human. He became truly man while remaining truly God. Jesus Christ is true God and true man" (CCC 464).

Jesus Christ took on a human nature. The eternal Son of God incarnate worked with human hands; he thought with a human mind. He acted with a human will, and loved with a human heart. He was like us in all things except sin (cf. CCC 470).

"Jesus Christ is true God and true man, in the unity of his divine person; for this reason he is the one and only mediator between God and man" (CCC 480).

"Jesus Christ possesses two natures, one divine and the other human, not confused, but united in the one person of God's Son" (CCC481).

Q. What is the significance of Jesus' entry into Jerusalem?

"Jesus' entry into Jerusalem manifested the coming of the kingdom that the King-Messiah was going to accomplish by the Passover of his Death and Resurrection. It is with the celebration of that entry on Palm Sunday that the Church's liturgy solemnly opens Holy Week" (CCC 560).

Q. What is the importance of the Death and Resurrection of Jesus?

"The Paschal mystery of Christ's cross and Resurrection stands at the centre of the Good News that the apostles, and the Church following them, are to proclaim to the world. God's saving plan was accomplished 'once and for all' by the redemptive death of His Son Jesus Christ" (CCC 571).

"Jesus' violent death was not the result of chance in an unfortunate coincidence of circumstances, but is part of the mystery of God's plan … (CCC 599).

At the Last Supper Jesus anticipated the free offering of his life.

"Jesus gave the supreme expression of his free offering of himself at the meal shared with the twelve Apostles 'on the night he was betrayed'. On the eve of his Passion, while still free, Jesus transformed this Last Supper with the apostles into the memorial of his voluntary offer to the Father for the salvation of people: 'This is my body which is *given* (handed over) for you.' 'This is my blood of the covenant, which is *poured out* for many for the forgiveness of sins" (CCC 610).

The agony at Gethsemane

"The cup of the New Covenant, which Jesus anticipated when he offered himself at the Last Supper, is afterwards accepted by him from his Father's hands in his agony in the garden at Gethsemane, making himself 'obedient unto death'. Jesus prays: 'My Father, if it be possible, let this cup pass from me...' Thus he expresses the horror that death represented for his human nature. Like ours, his human nature is destined for eternal life; but unlike ours, it is perfectly exempt from sin, the cause of death. Above all, his human nature has been assumed by the divine person of the 'Author of life', the 'Living One'. By accepting in his human will that the Father's will be done, he accepts his death as redemptive, for 'he himself bore our sins in his body on the tree'" (CCC 612).

Q. What is the meaning of the Resurrection of Jesus for us?

"The Resurrection of Jesus is the crowning truth of our faith in Christ, a faith believed and lived as the central truth by the first Christian community; handed on as fundamental by Tradition; established by the documents of the New Testament; and

preached as an essential part of the Paschal mystery along with the cross:
Christ is risen from the dead!
Dying, he conquered death;
to the dead, he has given life" (CCC 638).

"The Paschal mystery has two aspects: by his death, Christ liberates us from sin; by his Resurrection, he opens for us the way to a new life. This new life is above all *justification* that reinstates us in God's grace, 'so that as Christ was raised from the dead by the glory of the Father, we too might walk in the newness of life" (CCC 654).

Q. Was the resurrection of Jesus the same as the daughter of Jairus?

"Christ's Resurrection was not a return to earthly life, as was the case with the raisings from the dead that he had performed before Easter: Jairus' daughter, the young man of Naim, Lazarus. These actions were miraculous events, but the persons miraculously raised returned by Jesus' power to ordinary earthly life. At some particular moment they would die again. Christ's Resurrection is essentially different. In his risen body he passes from the state of death to another life beyond time and space. At Jesus' Resurrection his body is filled with the power of the Holy Spirit: he shares the divine life in his glorious state, so that St. Paul can say that Christ is 'the man of heaven'" (CCC646).

Additional Theological Notes

The Paschal Mystery
It is here that we make the connection with the **Eucharistic mystery** and the **new covenant.** At the Last Supper, Jesus changed the Jewish paschal meal from the offering of an external sacrifice – an animal, the paschal lamb – to the offering and **handing over of himself in love.** This is the radical change from the **old** covenant to the **new** covenant – not the blood of an animal (a lamb or goat or calf or heifer) but **his own blood** (Jesus' blood): "This cup **is the new covenant in my blood**" ... "**the blood of the new and everlasting covenant ....**" It is certainly striking how the Church, with a profoundly Christian instinct, on Holy Thursday – the day we celebrate the Institution of the Eucharist and of the Christian Priesthood – chooses for its Solemn Liturgy the gospel of the **Washing of the Feet** (Jn. 13:1-15). This is **not** the lesson merely of humble, selfless service **but the entire** DRAMA OF REDEMPTION, exactly parallel to the mystery of Christ's self-emptying, self-gift and self-surrender in love of CROSS AND RESURRECTION in the Pauline hymn **Philippines 2:5-11.** It is also in the second reading from **1 Corinthians 11: 23-26** which is Paul's account of the Institution of the Eucharist (**all** are centred on the Greek verb which means handing-over self).

At the Last Supper Jesus, with his heart full of love, opened that heart and shared with his beloved disciples and, through them, with all of us who were going to be his disciples down the centuries, his promise of pouring out his own Spirit. When his disciples were distraught at the fact that he was going to leave them, he assured and reassured them: "I must go. If I do not go, I cannot send the Spirit. I must go so that I can send the Spirit" (cf. Jn. 14:27-28; 16:6-7).

As disciples of Jesus Christ, we all have to go through our own Paschal mystery. We shall have our own way of the cross. Certainly, that is never the end of the road: there is, in Christ Jesus, resurrection for each of us too. We shall experience the power of Christ's resurrection. But while we are on the road carrying the cross, we need the comfort, counsel and consolation which the Spirit of God will give us. He will be our friend, our comfort and our consolation. The second meaning of that word 'Paraclete' is, as we have said, 'Advocate'. The Spirit will be our advocate not only before God, but before men and women who will resist and oppose God's call and work of salvation. The Spirit will be the one who will speak for us as our 'Advocate'. We recall Jesus telling his disciples: "You will be hailed before courts and judges. Do not worry about what you have got to say. If you trust in the Lord, the Spirit of God himself will be speaking through your lips" (cf. Mk. 13:9-11; Mt. 10:17-20; Lk. 12:11-12). He will be our advocate before the powers of the world, the powers of darkness.

The Risen Jesus

Jesus gives us in all these promises the assurance that the Spirit that he and his Father will send is the Spirit of Truth, the Comforter, the Advocate. Now the Risen Jesus actually fulfilled this promise, the promise we have had in the Last Supper discourse in the gospel of St. John, chapters 14, 15 and 16. The actual gift of the Spirit was brought by the Risen Jesus when he appeared to his disciples who, for fear of the Jews, had locked themselves behind closed doors. They were all huddled together under one roof, yet there was among them no community. It is not because persons are huddled together under one roof that there is necessarily community. The disciples had lost faith in Jesus – the key to, and secret of, Christian community. They thought everything was over; their world and worldly hopes were shattered by the death of Jesus on the cross. Afraid of the Jews, they locked themselves behind closed doors. And Jesus broke through these closed doors and closed hearts – the Risen Jesus – and said: "Peace be with you". Then he added: "Receive the Holy Spirit". He had earlier promised them the Spirit. Now he gives them that Spirit, the Spirit of peace and reconciliation. For the Risen Jesus continued: "Whose sins you will forgive, they are forgiven them whose sins you retain, they are retained" (cf. Jn. 20:21-23). The Spirit of Peace and Reconciliation!

Herbert Alphonso SJ

4.4 Jesus, the Saviour

> Know that Jesus is truly God and, as man, truly human.
> Reflect on what this means for us.

Jesus, truly God and truly human

Note for Teachers: *This is the most important module in the Book so it is essential to devote as much time as possible to all the key learning objectives – together they form the basis of our Christian faith and life. If pupils could make a presentation of this module to their parents just before Easter it will help them to deepen their knowledge and understanding, enable them to become religiously literate and give them an experience of mission by passing on the Faith.*

Starting point
Explain to pupils that we are now going to explore the mystery of the Incarnation, that is, that Jesus is truly God and as man, truly human. This is a mystery which we accept in faith.

Note: use the following when appropriate: **LENT** - Explain that the first day of Lent is called 'Ash Wednesday' because on this day we go to church to receive ashes from the priest. The priest makes the sign of the cross on our foreheads with the ashes. When he does this, he invites us to **repent** for the wrongs we have done and to live the Gospel.

PPP: Lent (CD ROM).

Pupil's Book pages 58 and 60.
Explain that one of the greatest mysteries of our faith is that Jesus is truly God and as man, truly human. It is through Jesus that we come to know what God is like.

PPP: Jesus true God and true Man – show part 1 – 'Jesus is truly human'. This is helpful to recap at the end of the lesson and at the beginning of the next lesson before going on to part 2 - 'Jesus is truly God'.

Additional activity
Invite pupils to work in pairs to prepare to explain to visitors what they are learning in their RE lesson:
    a) one explains that Jesus is truly human with examples;
    b) the other that he is truly God with examples;
    c) both share that this is a mystery which we believe in faith.

SMART notebook: Glossary

Pause to reflect
Have a quiet time when pupils can think about what they have been learning in the lesson. Allow time for them to ask questions before finishing.

Holy Week

**Know about Jesus' entry to Jerusalem.
Think about the importance of Holy Week for us.**

Jesus enters Jerusalem

Starting point – make links
For the three years of Jesus' public life the disciples had been attracted by his personality, his goodness, his teaching and by his miraculous powers.
They had seen him:

- feed 5,000 people with five loaves and two fish;
- cure the paralysed man;
- restore sight to the blind;
- cure the lepers;
- change water into wine.

Some of them even had lofty expectations and asked to be given a place of honour (Mk. 10:35-38). However one day, when the disciples were all with Jesus he said to them: "The Son of Man is about to be handed over to those who will kill him …" The disciples became very sad.

Jesus was referring to the growing hostility between himself and the Jewish leaders of the time *(this has nothing to do with the Jews today)*. The leaders saw Jesus as a threat. They were worried because they were not sure who he was and how he might harm their Jewish faith.

Read 'The Messiah enters Jerusalem' (Mark 11:1-11).

Listen to the audio recording '**The Donkey Owner**' (CD ROM).

 WS: The Donkey (CD ROM).

 PPP: Jesus enters Jerusalem
PPP: Palm Sunday in Church (CD ROM).

Explain that Passion Sunday is sometimes called Palm Sunday. Every year all over the world, the Church re-lives the events which happened over 2,000 years ago. Passion Sunday is the beginning of Holy Week.

 Reflection and Song: 'Hosanna to the Lord' & 'Sing Hosanna', CD More Stories & Songs of Jesus, available from McCrimmons Publishing.

Holy Thursday

**Understand what happened on Holy Thursday.
Reflect on how we can show our love for Jesus.**

The Last Supper

Starting point
Explain to the pupils that Holy Week is very special for all Christians.
Recap on how different groups felt about Jesus' entry into Jerusalem: the people; the
Religious Leaders; the Political Leaders.

On **Spy Wednesday**, Judas Iscariot plotted with the Sanhedrin, (Jewish High
Council), to hand Jesus over to them for thirty pieces of silver. That day they
planned to capture Jesus.

Holy Thursday or *Maundy* Thursday – the word *Maundy* comes from the command
(mandate) given by Jesus at the Last Supper that we should love one another.

PPP: **'The Meaning of the Last Supper'** (CD ROM).
PPP: **'The Meaning of the New Covenant'** (CD ROM).

WS page 64: Passover - Last Supper - Eucharist.

Explain: Jesus shares his thoughts with his close disciples: "You are the men who
have stood by me faithfully in my trials … ." Then he told Peter that Satan will
tempt him – Peter boasts that he will never let Jesus down. "I would be ready to go
to prison with you and to death", he said. Jesus replied, "I tell you, Peter, by the
time the cock crows today you will have denied three times that you know me."
(Lk. 22:28-34)

WS page 66: Peter lets Jesus down.

Pupil's Book page 65 Activity: Holy Week Diary (WS Outline on CD ROM). Use as
a plenary at the end of each lesson in Holy Week.

Additional activity
Role-play in groups of three.
One of you is a journalist and the others are James and John.
The journalist interviews:
  • John about what happened at the Last Supper and
  • James about Gethsemane.

Prayer
Jesus, we believe in you: increase our faith;
Jesus, we hope in you: always be our very close friend;
Jesus, we love you, show us how to live a good life.

Good Friday

Know what happened on Good Friday.
Reflect on the suffering of Jesus.

The Death of Jesus

Starting point

Help pupils to make connections between the events from Holy Thursday to Good Friday:

- After the Last Supper, Jesus and his disciples went to the Garden of Gethsemane.
- Jesus was arrested in the garden.
- He was taken to the house of Caiaphas, the High Priest.
- He was questioned before the High Priest and the Sanhedrin, the supreme Council of Jews.
- The trial was rigged. Jesus was found guilty because they were jealous of him and feared that he might make himself king. See Pupil's Book page 68.

Jesus' death

Explain that it is almost impossible for us to imagine the suffering that Jesus experienced on Good Friday. His disciples ran away and three times Peter had denied knowing him. *It will help to take pupils to church to make the Stations of the Cross or use the PPP on the CD ROM.*

PPP: Stations of the Cross (CD ROM). Allow time for pupils to reflect in silence after each station.

Additional activity

Give a brief outline of what happened to Jesus on Good Friday.
What do Christians do on Good Friday because of their belief and love for Jesus?
[Many people make the Stations of the Cross and/or go to the Good Friday Liturgy, see PPP on CD ROM].

PPP: Good Friday Liturgy in Church.

SMART notebook: Holy Week

PPP: Mary, Mother of Jesus: sorrow and joy
The disciples fled except for John. He remained with Mary at the foot of the cross. While Mary's heart was pierced with suffering she trusted God. She remembered all that God had done for her and hoped in Him.

Plenary: Update the Holy Week diary.

Death on a Cross – Why?

> Begin to understand why Jesus died on a cross.
> Think about what this means for us.

Why did Jesus die on a cross?

Notes for Teachers: Theological truths in Genesis
- *God created man and woman out of love.*
- *He created them in a state of holiness, which means, in a relationship of friendship with Him.*
- *God created them in His own image and likeness.*
- *He gave them the gift of freedom because He wanted them to be free to love Him.*
- *However, our 'first parents', whom the writers of Genesis call Adam and Eve, were tempted by the Evil One; they abused their God-given gift of freedom to turn against their Creator and disobey His command.*
- *By turning against God, they lost their original friendship and happiness with Him.*
- *God intended His original plan of one-ness with Him for all human beings, but the whole of human history was marked by the original fault freely committed by our first parents.*

Starting point

Explain to pupils that in order to understand why Jesus died on the cross we have to go back to the beginning when God created the world. The people of the Old Testament wanted to know about the creation of the universe so, in order to help them, the writers of Genesis used a mythical (symbolic) representation of humankind.

Notes to share with Pupils: Right back at the beginning of the time when human beings first lived on earth, they turned away from God. After that, people couldn't find their way back to Him – couldn't be part of God's family, unless God helped them. The story of the first couple, whom the writers of Genesis call Adam and Eve, helps us to understand what happened.

When Jesus, the Son of God, came to be with us, he made a way back to God's family for us through his death, resurrection and his ascension into heaven. He was fully human, was tempted as we are, but he resisted and even died on a cross. Through his own life, he showed his followers what it meant to love God perfectly and to do His will. We have that example of his way of life before us today.

PPP: Why did Jesus dies on a cross? (CD ROM)

Read the story of Itsuo and Takeo, two Japanese boys. (TB 67 & CD ROM)

The Resurrection of Jesus

Understand what happened on Easter Sunday.
Reflect on the importance of the resurrection of Jesus for us.

Jesus appears to Mary of Magdala

Starting point
Explain to the pupils that the resurrection of Jesus from the dead is the most important event in the whole Bible and it is of enormous importance for us - now we have to find out why.

PPP: Mary, Mother of Jesus: sorrow and joy.

Pupil's Book: Jesus appears to Mary of Magdala.

- What was the first thing Mary noticed? *(Stone rolled away).*
- Who do you think moved it? *(Gospel does not tell us, we assume it was by divine power).*
- Why do you think Mary did not recognise Jesus? *(It was the Risen Jesus and people recognised him in the things he did and said – but it was not easy at first to recognise his physical appearance – remind pupils of the disciples on the road to Emmaus, they recognised Jesus in the breaking of bread, PB 3 pp. 74-75; Thomas recognised Jesus when he saw the wounds of the nails in his hands and feet PB 3 p.78.)*
- What was it that helped Mary to recognise Jesus?
- Imagine you had the chance to interview Mary – what questions would you want to ask her?

PPP: The Resurrection - Jesus appears to Mary of Magdala (CD ROM).

Explain: Jesus rose from the dead and showed that death was not the end for him and it is not the end for us. Jesus has said: "Whoever believes in me will live, even though he/she died" (Jn. 11:25). If we receive the sacraments and follow the teaching of Jesus, our physical death will just be a *passing over* to a new life with Jesus. (For information on the sacraments see Pupil's Book 3, pages 10-18; 48-53; 54-66).

ICT Link
www.cptryon.org.prayer/child/lent/holywk01.html

Prayer
Lord Jesus,
I give you my hands to do your work.
I give you my feet to go your way.
I give you my eyes to see as you do.
Above all, I give you myself that you may grow in me,
so that it is you, Lord Jesus, who live and work in me.

Passover – Last Supper – Eucharist

At the **Passover**, every Israelite family was to choose a perfect lamb to offer to God in sacrifice. They were to cook and eat the lamb with unleavened bread and bitter herbs. The blood of the lamb was to be put

on the doorposts to show where the Israelites were gathered. In this way the final plague which was to strike the land of Egypt would **pass over** them and the Israelites would be saved. This event is still celebrated today.

At the **Last Supper during the Passover feast**, Jesus gave himself, his own body and blood in the form of bread and wine instead of the Lamb. Jesus freely offered his life on the cross and gave himself in love to the Father as the most perfect sacrifice to save the world from its sins and to open the way to heaven for us.

At **Mass** (Eucharist), the same sacrifice that Jesus made when he handed over his life to the Father on the cross is made present again under the sacramental sign of bread and wine.

When the priest repeats the words that Jesus said at the Last Supper: *This is my body, this is my blood,* Jesus becomes truly present. We still have the bread and wine – but in faith Jesus is present.

Before Jesus gave his life for us, eternal life with the Father was closed to us because of sin and selfishness – sin and selfishness means that we think only of ourselves. Through his death and resurrection Jesus handed over his life for us, and this opened a new way to the Father for everyone.

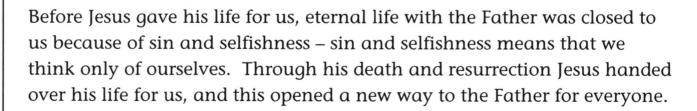

Activity

a) What is the difference between the Passover and the Last Supper?

b) What is the link between the Last Supper and the Mass?

The Paschal Mystery

The Paschal Mystery is the mystery of the passion, death and resurrection of Jesus.

Pupils will work in groups of two or three and prepare a Power Point presentation on the Paschal Mystery which they can show to all the parents and friends. They must also be ready to answer questions about it.

	Task	Help on pages	Pupils
1.	Jesus, truly human	58	
2.	Jesus, truly God	60-61	
3.	Passion Sunday	62-63	
4.	The Last Supper	64-65	
5.	Gethsemane	66	
6.	Peter's denials	67	
7.	Death of Jesus	68-69	
8.	Why Jesus died on a cross	70-71	
9.	Resurrection of Jesus	72	
10.	What the Resurrection means for us.	73	

Peter lets Jesus down

After Jesus had been arrested and taken away, the others followed at a distance. Peter went into the courtyard of the High Priest's house where Jesus' trial was being held.

Peter tells us what happened:

"It was a chilly night and they'd lit a fire there. I couldn't hear what was going on inside, but I knew they were accusing Jesus of all sorts of things that just weren't true. Suddenly, one of the maids looked straight at me and said to the other servants: "This man was with Jesus too - look!" I turned away, and told her she must have been mistaken. I was scared. What if they arrested me too? What if they threw me into prison - or worse? I moved away from the fire.

But then a man approached me. "I'm sure I saw you with him at the Temple this week," he claimed. I glared at him. "Not me!" I said, pulling my cloak around me. Perhaps I should just get out of here, I thought ... Jesus will be able to look after himself. I could go back to Galilee and take up where I left off, fishing in the lake. Ah, Galilee! I missed my home and my family and... "He's a Galilean!" someone called out to the others. "Just listen to his accent!" "Leave me alone!" I shouted. "I have no idea what you're talking about!"

At that moment, I heard the cock crow and remembered what Jesus had said to me over supper. "Before the cock crows, Peter," he'd told me,

"You'll have said three times that you don't know me." I'd insisted that he was wrong - that I'd never deny him. But he'd been right, hadn't he? When challenged, I'd said I hadn't known him. I felt really ashamed of myself and ran out of the courtyard, tears streaming down my face. How could he ever forgive me? I didn't deserve to be called his friend!" (*See Luke 22:54-62*)

1. Sometimes we have an 'argument' inside our minds. Our conscience might say, "You shouldn't have done that". We might say, "I couldn't help it." Write one speech bubble for Peter's conscience and one for his reply.

2. If you had met Peter after he heard the cock crow
   (a) What would you have said to him?
   (b) How would you have tried to help him?
   (c) What do you think Jesus would say to him?

Itsuo and Takeo

The Japanese Boys

When Fr. Pedro Arrupe, a Jesuit priest, was teaching in a missionary school in Japan, he told the children about the enormous sacrifice Jesus made to save us from sin and to make it possible for us to enjoy eternal life with him in heaven.

He explained that to show our love for Jesus we should try to make little sacrifices, like being kind to someone when we find it difficult or saying 'sorry' even though we might still feel a bit annoyed with someone.

Father and the children agreed to set up a little cardboard box which looked like a moneybox, so that they could drop their offerings of good deeds into it.

One day, two boys had a violent argument. Each of them went to an opposite corner of the classroom and they stayed there all afternoon with sulky looks on their faces.

Saa, a young girl, told Father that Itsuo and Takeo had had a big row and they were both in a very bad mood. Everybody in the class knew about it. Father was curious to see the result of this dispute because there was a very special friendship between these two young boys.

Itsuo was eight years old and he was allowed to walk around the streets on his own, but Takeo was only five and needed Itsuo to take him home after school.

Now, what were they going to do? They had quarrelled. It was getting late and they had to go home. Father said nothing but was watching to see what would happen. The other pupils were leaving, chatting happily – and the two opponents were still sulking.

While Father was chatting with a few stragglers, he could see Itsuo approaching little Takeo and saying something which he could not hear. But it must have been friendly, because Takeo gave him his hand. Without saying another word they left to go home together.

When all the children had left, Father opened the 'money-box' with its offerings and before burning them in front of the picture of the Sacred Heart of Jesus, he noticed one not signed, but he knew who had written it:

"It was for you, Jesus, that I made peace with Takeo, even though it was his fault and not mine. To give you consolation, I will take him home as if nothing has happened." Father was thrilled because this was a wonderful gift for Jesus.

4.5 The Early Christians

Religious Education Curriculum Directory
Catechism of the Catholic Church
"On the day of Pentecost when the seven weeks of Easter had come to an end, Christ's Passover is fulfilled in the outpouring of the Holy Spirit, manifested given and communicated as a divine person: of his fullness, Christ, the Lord pours out the Spirit in abundance" (CCC 731).

Attainment Target 1: Learning *about* the Catholic faith.
Attainment Target 2: Learning *from* the Catholic faith.

Key Learning Objectives

- Know that Jesus made Peter Head of the Church.
  - Think about what this means for all Christians.

- Know that the Church began at Pentecost.
  - Think about what the Holy Spirit is able to do.

- Know what happened to Stephen and Saul.
  - Reflect on how God brings good out of evil.

- Know about the challenges of being an apostle.
  - Reflect on how God worked through Paul and Silas.

- Know about Paul's missionary journeys.
  - Reflect on Paul's faith and courage.

- Know about the teaching of the Apostles.
  - Reflect on how this teaching helps us today.

Theological Notes

Q. What does Jesus' resurrection mean for us?
By his resurrection, Christ "opens for us the way to a new life. This new life is above all justification that reinstates us in God's grace, 'so that as Christ was raised from the dead by the glory of the Father, we too might walk in newness of life…'" (CCC 654).

"Finally, Christ's Resurrection – and the risen Christ himself – is the principle and source of our future resurrection: 'Christ has been raised from the dead, the first fruits of those who have fallen asleep . . . For as in Adam all die, so also in Christ shall all be made alive.' The risen Christ lives in the hearts of his faithful while they await that fulfilment.

In Christ, Christians 'have tasted . . . the powers of the age to come' and their lives are swept up by Christ into the heart of divine life, so that they may "live no longer for themselves but for him who for their sake dies and was raised" (CCC 655). "Christ, 'the first born from the dead' (*Col* 1:18), is the principle of our own resurrection, even now by the justification of our souls (cf. *Rom* 6:4), and one day by the new life he will impart to our bodies (cf. *Rom* 8:11)" (CCC 658).

Q. What is the significance of Jesus making Peter head of the Church?

"Simon Peter holds the first place in the college of the Twelve; Jesus entrusted a unique mission to him. Through revelation from the Father, Peter had confessed: 'You are the Christ, the Son of the living God.' Our Lord then declared to him: 'You are Peter, and on this rock I will build my Church, and the gates of Hades will not prevail against it.' Christ, the 'living stone', thus assures his Church, built on Peter, of victory over the powers of death. Because of the faith he confessed Peter will remain the unshakeable rock of the Church. His mission will be to keep this faith from every lapse and to strengthen his brothers in it" (CCC 552).

"Jesus entrusted a specific authority to Peter: 'I will give you the keys of the kingdom of heaven, and whatever you bind on earth shall be bound in heaven, and whatever you loose on earth shall be loosed in heaven.' The 'power of the keys' designates authority to govern the house of God, which is the Church. Jesus, the Good Shepherd, confirmed this mandate after his Resurrection: 'Feed my sheep.' The power to 'bind and loose' connotes the authority to absolve sins, to pronounce doctrinal judgements, and to make disciplinary decisions in the Church. Jesus entrusted this authority to the Church through the ministry of the apostles and in particular through the ministry of Peter, the only one to whom he specifically entrusted the keys of the kingdom" (CCC 553).

Q. What happened in Jerusalem at Pentecost? (Acts 2)

"On the day of Pentecost when the seven weeks of Easter had come to an end, Christ's Passover is fulfilled in the outpouring of the Holy Spirit, manifested, given, and communicated as a divine person: of his fullness, Christ, the Lord, pours out the Spirit in abundance" (CCC 731). "On that day, the Holy Trinity is fully revealed. Since that day, the kingdom announced by Christ has been open to those who believe in him: in the humility of the flesh and in faith, they are already in the communion of the Holy Trinity.

By his coming, which never ceases, the Holy Spirit causes the world to enter into the 'last days', the time of the Church, the kingdom already inherited though not yet consummated" (CCC 732). The Holy Spirit, whom Christ the head pours out on his members, builds, animates, and sanctifies the Church. She is the sacrament of the Holy Trinity's communion with us.

Q. In what sense if the Holy Spirit God's gift?
"'God is Love' and love is His first gift, containing all others. 'God's love has been poured into our hearts through the Holy Spirit who has been given to us'" (CCC 733).

"Because we are dead or at least wounded through sin, the first effect of the gift of love is the forgiveness of our sins. The communion of the Holy Spirit in the Church restores to the baptised the divine likeness lost through sin" (CCC 734).

"God, then, gives us the 'pledge' or 'first fruits' of our inheritance: the very life of the Holy Trinity, which is to love as 'God [has] loved us'. This love (the 'charity' of 1 Cor. 13) is the source of the new life in Christ, made possible because we have received 'power' from the Holy Spirit" (CCC735).

"By this power of the Spirit, God's children can bear much fruit. He who has grafted us on to the true vine will make us bear 'the fruit of the Spirit: … love, joy, peace, patience, kindness, goodness, faithfulness, gentleness, self-control'. 'We live by the Spirit'; the more we renounce ourselves, the more we 'walk by the Spirit'" (CCC736).

Q. How were the disciples changed by the coming of the Holy Spirit at Pentecost?
Before the coming of the Spirit they locked themselves away for fear of the Jews. After it, they fearlessly proclaimed the gospel message even though they were persecuted for so doing (Acts 4 & 5), and had to face death (Acts 8 & 12).

Additional Theological Notes

Q. What was it that shattered Saul's most cherished dreams and turn him around completely – one hundred and eighty degrees – to make him the Paul we now know, the apostle of Jesus Christ?
"Breathing threats and murder against the disciples of the Lord", he (Saul) had official letters from the Jewish high-priest to round up and bring, bound and fettered, from Damascus men and women "belonging to the Way" – that is, Christians. When, in zealous pursuit of this purpose, he was journeying to and nearing Damascus, he was knocked to the ground by a blinding light; he heard a voice saying, "Saul, Saul, why do you persecute me? …I am Jesus whom you are persecuting; but rise and enter the city, and you will be told what you are to do". Led by the hand into Damascus, because he was blinded by the light which had knocked him to the ground, Saul was accosted while he was at prayer by a man sent to him by the Lord – Ananias – to whom the Lord had said categorically in the face of his protests that Saul was persecuting the Christians: "Go, for this man is a chosen instrument of mine to carry my name before the Gentiles and kings and the sons of Israel; for I will show him how much he must suffer for the sake of my name".

Ananias did as the Lord had told him to do: laying his hands on Saul, he said, "Brother Saul, the Lord Jesus who appeared to you on the road by which you came, has sent me that you may regain your sight and be filled with the Holy Spirit". Saul regained his sight, rose and was baptised; he took food and was strengthened.

In this way began the apostolic adventure of Paul, "the apostle of the nations". It is this intensely personal encounter with the Lord Jesus, in which he receives his vocation, that he 'remembers' whenever he is in difficult challenging situations or at the crossroads of decision-making in the living out of his apostolic-missionary calling.

Q. What helped Paul to persevere when he was being persecuted?

Paul shares his profoundly personal secret in his letter to the Philippians. In Chapter 3: he begins verse 6 by enumerating all the 'fleshly' advantages he has as a Hebrew of the tribe of Benjamin, a Pharisee who outstripped other Pharisees in his fiery zeal and scrupulous observance of the law. Now, then, comes his profoundly personal secret: "But, whatever gain I had, I counted as loss for the sake of Christ. Indeed I count everything as loss because of the surpassing worth of **knowing Christ Jesus my Lord**" (Phil. 3:7-8a). In this word 'knowing', we have a first privileged glimpse into Paul's inner life-secret, for it is not a question here of mere intellectual or conceptual knowledge. In the Bible this word connotes interior and intimate knowledge, experiential knowledge, a knowledge of the heart, which signifies a deeply personal love relationship. No wonder, Paul continues to invite us into the inmost secret chambers of his inner being: "For **his** sake – that is for the sake of Christ Jesus my Lord – I have suffered the loss of all things and count them as refuse (rubbish and garbage) in order that I may gain Christ and be found in him, not having a righteousness of my own, based on law, but that which is through faith in Christ, the righteousness from God that depends on faith" (Phil. 3:8b-9).

What becomes clearer and clearer in Paul's sharing is that his inmost life-secret is his passionate love for the person of Christ Jesus which, in his consciousness, is only his active response to the passionate personal love Christ Jesus had for him in taking hold of him on his own road of life. To us, therefore, it is far from surprising that Paul depicts his life's aim as **"gaining Christ, and being found in Christ Jesus"**; this, he himself paraphrases as entering ever more deeply into the core of the person of Christ Jesus, by sharing intimately in Jesus Christ's own personal and essential mystery, which is his paschal mystery of death-resurrection. Paul's own paraphrase reads thus: "that I may know him (Christ Jesus) and the power of his resurrection, and may share his sufferings, becoming like him in his death, that if possible I may attain the resurrection from the dead" (Phil. 3:10-11).

Herbert Alphonso SJ

4.5 The Early Christians

Know that Jesus made Peter head of the Church.
Think about what this means for all Christians.

Jesus appears to the disciples

Starting point
Listen to the recording: '**Jesus and his friends have breakfast on the beach**', CD 'More Stories & Songs of Jesus, Disc 2 no. 7 (Available from McCrimmons Publishing) As an alternative read John 21:1-13.

When pupils have done the activity in Pupil's Book page 74 listen to the recording: '**Jesus asks, 'Do you love Me'** CD Disc 2 no. 9 as above.
Make links with Peter's triple denial.

Explain: Jesus makes Peter head of the Church on earth. He became the first Pope and with the other apostles they formed the Church. The 'lambs and the sheep' are all the baptised Christians.

Jesus passed on his mission, power and authority to the apostles (Matt. 28:16-20). They have passed it on to the Church today. Unlike a government in a country, all power in the Church comes from Jesus. The Catholic Church traces its origin back to the time of the Apostles. So today in the Church we have:
- the Pope (successor of Peter)
- the Bishops (successors of the Apostles)
- the Priests (ordained ministers)
- the People of God (all baptised Christians)

So the Pope, bishops and priests have the power to forgive sins and to celebrate the sacraments. They keep the Church free from error in matters of faith and morals. All of us, because we have received the Sacrament of Baptism, have a responsibility to witness to Jesus by the way we live.

PPP: Peter's progress.
PPP: Hot-seating Peter.

Plenary: discuss
- Why is it important for us to know that the Catholic Church goes back to the time of the Apostles?   *(Because we understand it is the true Church founded by Jesus).*
- What power did the Apostles receive from Jesus? How does that power help us today? *(Teach the Word of God and celebrate the sacraments. We can be sure that the teaching of the Church is based on the teaching of Jesus).*
- Is it important to know that the Pope is the successor of St. Peter? Why?
  (Because Jesus himself entrusted his Church to Peter and this authority has been handed on to all the Popes who came after Peter).

Pentecost

Know that the Church began at Pentecost.
Think about what the Holy Spirit is able to do.

The Ascension

Starting point

Explain that we must listen very carefully while we explore what Jesus told the Apostles before he went back to heaven.

We know that when somebody dies, they leave us completely. If they have led a very good life they have gone to heaven to be with Jesus. But Jesus says of his death: **"I go away, and I will come to you."** It is by going away that he comes back again. His going brings about a completely new and greater way of being present. We know it is very hard to understand but it is true.

By dying, Jesus enters into the love of the Father. His dying is an act of love. Love is immortal – it never dies. His going away is transformed into a new coming, into a new form of presence which reaches deeper and deeper and does not come to an end.

In the Sacrament of Baptism, Jesus enters our life through the door of our heart. This is the reality of Baptism: he, the Risen Jesus, comes; he comes and joins our life to his life and draws us into his very great love. We become one with him. (Cf. *I Believe in One God*, pp. 127 & 129, Pope Benedict XVI)

WATCH **PPP: Meaning of the Ascension** -to help explain the text above (CD ROM).

Pentecost:
Jesus had told the apostles three things:
- to go back to Jerusalem;
- to stay in the city until the Holy Spirit (his Spirit) came;
- to be his witnesses so that everyone would know that he had risen from the dead.

Read Acts 2:1-13. Help the pupils to understand the powerful effect the Spirit of Jesus had on the apostles. They immediately felt, brave, strong and ready for anything. Now they understood what Jesus had taught them so they rushed out to spread the Good News.

Additional activity: Draw a candle to show how you want the light of Jesus to shine through you. Around the rays of the candle write words or phrases to describe what you will do.

Song: Share the Light, CD *Share the Light*, Bernadette Farrell
www.viewpoint24.co.uk

Prayers to the Holy Spirit (CD ROM).

Stephen and Saul

Know what happened to Stephen and Saul.
Reflect on how God brings good out of evil.

Stephen

 ### Starting point
Read Pupil's Book 79 then, **pause to reflect**: imagine Stephen surrounded by a great angry crowd. He realises he is on his own. There is no-one on his side. He understands that things are turning out badly for him.

What choices did Stephen have now?

(He could have been afraid, intimidated and uncertain and said 'sorry', but not mean what he said.

He could have told his enemies that they were right, knowing they were stronger.)

What did happen?

(Stephen experienced the Spirit of Jesus working in him. He was "filled with the Holy Spirit, gazed into heaven and saw the glory of God and Jesus standing at God's right hand.")

 WS: Stephen's Speech (TB p. 78 & CD ROM) or pupils read Acts 7:55-60 and 8:1-3.
- What did Stephen say that made the crowd stone him?
- What did Stephen say to Jesus?
- What did he ask Jesus to do for those stoning him?
- What did Saul do?

 PPP: Stoning of Stephen (CD ROM)

Discuss: In what ways did Stephen's belief in Jesus shape his life?
Think about his:
- courage;
- vision;
- faithfulness;
- and what it was that identified him most of all with Jesus at the hour of his death. *(He forgave those who stoned him).*

 SMART notebook: Stephen and Saul – spider diagrams.

PPP: Conversion of Saul (CD ROM)

 ### Additional activity
Imagine you are Paul. You are going to see Peter and the apostles for the first time.
   a) What do you think the apostles would say when they saw you come into the room?
   b) What would be the first thing you would say to Peter?
   c) What would you offer to do to spread the Good News?

Paul and Silas

Know about the challenges of being an apostle.
Reflect on how God worked through Paul and Silas.

Paul in Damascus

Starting point
Re-cap on Paul's experience on the road to Damascus:
He was totally blinded by the light from the sky.
His friends had to take him to the city.
A Christian named Ananias came to him, laid hands on him and his sight returned.
Paul believed in Jesus and was baptised.

Additional activity
Hot-seating: Pupils take turns to be Paul. (The following questions are on the CD ROM)
Imagine that television existed in the time of Paul. Lots of reporters arrive in
Damascus to interview him.
Here are some questions, pupils can add their own.

- What is your name?
- What happened on the road to Damascus?
- What did the voice sound like?
- What message did the voice give you?
- What do you think the message means?
- Do you think it was your imagination? Why? Why not?
- How do you feel now about the way you were persecuting the Christians?
- What are your plans now?

Explain that to everyone's amazement, Paul begins preaching the Gospel
everywhere. His witness is so powerful that his old allies plot to kill him. Read Pupil's
Book p.82.

SMART Notebook: Peter and Paul

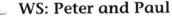

WS: Peter and Paul

Paul and Silas
When Paul and Silas spoke about Jesus in Philippi, they were falsely charged, beaten
and imprisoned. They spent the time praying and growing closer to God. (Acts16:25)

The miraculous deliverance of Paul and Silas (Acts 16:23-35)
Give the pupils a copy of the scripture text (copy on CD ROM). They work in small
groups and plan a role-play and then present it.

Plenary: How did God bring good out of evil for Paul and Silas?

The Cost of Discipleship

> Know about Paul's missionary journeys.
> Reflect on Paul's faith and courage.

A Disciple

Starting point

Take time to think about the things Jesus said to his disciples about being a follower of his. In what ways have his words come true for Paul? Ask the pupils if they have heard about any parts of the world where Christians are persecuted today. What can we do to help them? *(Pray)*.

Paul's Faith and Courage

Paul's life has been transformed – Jesus has become everything for him. He is ready to give his life for Jesus. He lives his life constantly in union with Jesus so that he says: **"It is no longer I who live, but Jesus Christ who lives in me"** (Gal. 2:20).

Paul does suffer and he feels it intensely but nothing would stop him spreading the Good News about the life, death and resurrection of Jesus. Why? Because he wants everyone to know the truth about Jesus and to share eternal life with him.

Map of Paul's journey's and notes for teachers (CD ROM).

Pause to reflect: What can we do to share the Good News with other people?

Shared prayer:

Take the first part of the following prayer and invite the pupils to complete it with their thoughts.

a. Jesus, give me your strength, *(because sometimes things get tough, and I am ready to give up)*.

b. Jesus, give me your love, *(because sometimes people hurt me, and I am tempted to hate them)*.

c. Jesus, give me your courage, *(because sometimes I am under pressure and it is hard to do what is right)*.

d. Jesus, give me yourself, *(because my heart was made for you, and it will not rest until it rests in you)*.

The Teaching of the Apostles

Know some of the teaching of the Apostles.
Reflect on how this teaching helps us today.

God's Spirit at Work

 Starting point

For several months now we have been learning about the life and teaching of Jesus and the apostles. These are wonderful opportunites for us to grow closer to Jesus and to share the Good News with others.

Look at the teaching of the apostles in your Book page 89.
What else can you remember about Jesus – his miracles, parables, etc?
How are we going to 'live it out', put it into practice?
Work in small groups to come up with ideas.

 Additional activities

1. Suggest what you can do to be a true follower of Jesus.

   (The following are only suggestions for pupils who need help).

   - *Give an hour on Sunday to go to Mass to be with Jesus.*
   - *Spend ten minutes praying to Jesus before going to bed.*
   - *Give time to help your parents or tidy your things.*
   - *Think of some ways to help poorer people.*

2. Look again the teaching of Jesus (Pupil's Book pages 50-52) and the apostles.
   Make a 'thinking map' to show how some of this teaching could shape the lives of pupils in:
   - the playground;
   - the classroom;
   - at home.

 Plenary - Discuss:

Invite pupils to share what they have learnt this term about the lives of the apostles.
   - What was the most interesting event?
   - Which apostle do you think was the most courageous? Why?
   - Which one was the most inspiring? Why?
   - Which one is likely to help us when we make big mistakes? Why?
   - Think of ways to share what you have learned with the rest of the school.

Stephen's Speech
(Summary of Acts 7:1-54)

Stephen began his speech to the Jewish High Council by outlining God's call to Abraham. Then he went on to the birth of Isaac and the birth of Isaac's son Jacob.

Jacob's name was changed to Israel by God. His twelve sons became leaders of the twelve tribes of Israel. They were called the Israelites.

Next Stephen told them how Joseph, one of the twelve sons, was betrayed by his brothers. Later on, this persecuted and rejected brother, Joseph, was the one to save all the others

Stephen reminded them that the Israelites were slaves in Egypt. God took pity on them and chose Moses to be their leader. It was Moses, through the power of God, who led the Israelites out of slavery into the wilderness.

While they were in the wilderness, Moses went up the mountain to talk to God and the Israelites turned their back on him. They made a golden calf and offered sacrifice to it.

Finally, Stephen recalled how God had led the Israelites into the Promised Land. Then Stephen paused, looked right at the Council and said:

"You stubborn people, with your pagan hearts and pagan ears, you are always resisting the Holy Spirit, just as your ancestors used to do. Can you name a single prophet your ancestors never persecuted? In the past, they killed those who foretold the coming of the Just One, and now you have become his betrayers, his murderers. You who had the Law brought to you by angels are the very ones who have not kept it" (7: 51 – 54).

They were furious when they heard this and ground their teeth at him. They took what he had said as blasphemy and stoned him to death.

Activities

1. What were the most important events that Stephen mentioned in his speech?
2. Why do you think the High Council were furious with him?

Easter Liturgy

Teacher: Today, let us celebrate our belief that Jesus rose from the dead, that he is alive and he is with us.

Jesus, Risen from the Dead

Easter Sunday

A reading from the Gospel of Luke

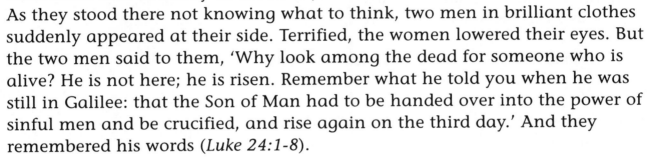

On the first day of the week, at the first sign of dawn, they (the women) went to the tomb with the spices they had prepared. They found that the stone had been rolled away from the tomb, but on entering discovered that the body of the Lord Jesus was not there. As they stood there not knowing what to think, two men in brilliant clothes suddenly appeared at their side. Terrified, the women lowered their eyes. But the two men said to them, 'Why look among the dead for someone who is alive? He is not here; he is risen. Remember what he told you when he was still in Galilee: that the Son of Man had to be handed over into the power of sinful men and be crucified, and rise again on the third day.' And they remembered his words (*Luke 24:1-8*).

Group 1 Jesus, you are risen from the dead.
Response Jesus, we believe it.

Group 2 Jesus, you promised to be with us always.
Response Jesus, we believe it.

Group 3 Jesus, you are present in the Blessed Sacrament.
Response Jesus, we believe it.

Group 4 Jesus, you have promised us eternal life.
Response Jesus, we believe it.

Group 5 Jesus, you have promised to send us the Holy Spirit.
Response Jesus, we believe it.

Teacher: Jesus, today, we ask you to increase our faith, hope and love in you.

[Finish with Easter song or hymn]

4.6 The Church

Religious Education Curriculum Directory
Catechism of the Catholic Church
"The Church is the family of God, the People that God gathers in the whole world. The Church is the communion of Christ's disciples, brought together in Christ its Head by the Holy Spirit. It is the Body of Christ, the Temple of the Spirit. As the People of God, the Church is drawn into Christ's praise of the Father and Christ's mission in the world" (CCC 751-757 abridged).

Attainment Target 1: Learning *about* the Catholic faith.
Attainment Target 2: Learning *from* the Catholic faith.

Key Learning Objectives

- Understand that the Church is a family.
  - Be aware that we belong to the Church.

- Understand that the Church is 'good news' for people.
  - Be aware that this 'good news' is also for us.

- Know about the different seasons in the Church's year.
  - Think about why these times are important for us.

- Know about the Communion of Saints and the Holy Souls.
  - Be aware of how they can help us.

- Know about God's call to individuals.
  - Reflect on their responses.

- Deepen our understanding of Mary.
  - Reflect on how she can help all of us.

Theological Notes

The Church is Apostolic
"The Church is apostolic because she is founded on the apostles, in three ways:
i) she was and remains built on 'the foundation of the apostles', the witnesses chosen and sent on mission by Christ himself;
ii) with the help of the Spirit dwelling in her, the Church keeps and hands on the teaching, the 'good deposit', the salutary words she has heard from the apostles;
iii) she continues to be taught, sanctified and guided by the apostles until Christ's return, through their successors in pastoral office: the college of bishops, 'assisted by priests, in union with the successor of Peter, the Church's supreme pastor'" (CCC 857).

Q. What does it mean to say that the Church is the 'People of God'?

"It is the People of God: God is not the property of any one people. But He acquired a people for Himself from those who previously were not a people: 'a chosen race, a royal priesthood, a holy nation'" (CCC 782).

Q. How does one become a member of the Church?

"One becomes a *member* of the Church, this people of God, not by a physical birth, but by being 'born anew', a birth 'of water and the Spirit', that is, by faith in Christ, and Baptism" (CCC 782).

Q. What does it mean to say that the Church is the Body of Christ?

"From the beginning, Jesus associated his disciples with his own life, revealed the mystery of the Kingdom to them and gave them a share in his mission, joy and sufferings. Jesus spoke of a still more intimate communion between him and those who would follow him: 'Abide in me, and I in you … I am the vine, you are the branches.' And he proclaimed a mysterious and real communion between his own body and ours: 'He who eats my flesh and drinks my blood abides in me, and I in him'" (CCC 787).

"When his visible presence was taken from them, Jesus did not leave his disciples orphans. He promised to remain with them until the end of time; he sent them his Spirit. As a result communion with Jesus has become, in a way, more intense: 'By communicating his Spirit, Christ mystically constitutes as his body those brothers of his who are called together from every nation'" (CCC 788).

Q. In what way is Mary mother of the Church?

"Mary's role in the Church is inseparable from her union with Christ and flows directly from it. 'This union of the mother with the Son in the work of salvation is made manifest from the time of Christ's virginal conception up to his death'; it is manifest above all at the hour of his Passion" (CCC 964).

"After her Son's Ascension, Mary 'aided the beginning of the Church by her prayers.' In her association with the apostles and several women, 'we also see Mary by her prayers imploring the gift of the Spirit, who had already overshadowed her in the Annunciation'" (CCC 965).

Additional Theological Notes

Mary, Mother of the Church

The Annunciation (Lk. 1:26-38)

Through his messenger Gabriel, God breaks into Mary's life and calls her the highly favoured one, full of grace. Mary is troubled: she, full of grace, highly-favoured one? There must be some mistake! What could this mean? But she is assured, and reassured: 'Yes, God's favour is on **you**, Mary'. And then she begins what is really a process of discernment. "You are calling **me** to be the mother of the Messiah?" True, every Jewish young lady, every Jewish maiden could dream and live in the hope of being the mother of the Messiah. But Mary said immediately: "How can this be, since I have no relations with men? I have no sexual relations with any man. How can I be the mother of the Messiah?" She is told forthwith that man will have no part in this; God alone is going to do it all: "The power of the Most High will overshadow you, and the Spirit of God will work his miracle within you, so you will be Mother".

When Mary has heard that God is going to do it all, and is told that, as in the case of her cousin Elizabeth who was long past the age of child-bearing the latter would have a child, because nothing is impossible to God, Mary proffers her significant answer. Far from saying, 'All right, then, I will be the mother of the Messiah', she says, rather: "I am only a servant, a handmaid of the Lord: if God is going to do it all, be it done to me according to your (the messenger Gabriel's) word". Total active availability to the Word of God! Active openness to God's word, God's will, God's call! Such is how the mystery of Mary begins in Luke's Gospel.

The Visitation (Lk. 1:39-56)
Immediately after the Annunciation, we have the mystery of the Visitation – Mary's visit to her cousin Elizabeth. Mary goes out in haste; filled with the Word now, she goes out to dispense the Word and the graces of the Word. Her cousin, Elizabeth, is in need, and she rushes out to be of help, though she herself has now conceived. Let us note what Elizabeth says after the initial greetings; filled with the Holy Spirit, she exclaims: "Blessed are you because you have believed the Word of God". Mary is "blessed" because she "has believed the Word of God". Mary's mystery is the mystery of 'faith', mystery of 'availability to God's Word'.

Mary sings her 'Magnificat'. It is a marvellous symphony on the same theme of active availability to God and His Word. God is praised and glorified for richly blessing those who are open and available to Him and His Word. The hungry, namely, those who are open to God's Word, will be filled with good things; the rich, who are full of themselves, he will send empty away. He has pulled down from their thrones the mighty, that is, those who close themselves in on their self-sufficiency and resources of self; he has exalted the lowly and humble ones, those open-hearted and available.

The Birth of the Lord (Lk. 2:1-20)
What shines out resplendently of Mary's attitude in this account is her obedience and availability to God's will and Word. A young pregnant woman has to undertake the arduous journey all the way from Nazareth down to Bethlehem! But it is God who, in His Providence, has disposed all things through a proud emperor's decree to have all the inhabitants throughout his vast Roman empire register themselves in the place of their origin. And so, Mary and Joseph set out for far-away Bethlehem, the city of David, since Joseph belonged to the lineage of David; in other words, Mary and Joseph obey the emperor's decree. And when Mary has borne her child in a ramshackle stable, because there was no room for them in the

inn, and when the shepherds had come to adore the child Jesus and had gone away to make their discovery joyfully known to their friends and people, St. Luke loses no time in telling us immediately: "And Mary kept all these words in her heart and pondered over them". Again, Mary's openness and active availability to God's Word as if the Lukan Word of God would have no other message for us but this, on Mary and her mystery.

Presentation of the Child Jesus in the Temple (Lk. 2:22-35)
Mary and Joseph take Jesus to be presented in the Temple, forty days after his birth, according to the Law. Concentrating on the person and mystery of Mary, as we are now doing, we note that Mary is not just fulfilling the Mosaic Law. She is making the gift of herself with her Son, making the total gift of herself in active availability to God, His Word and His call for her. It is in this scene that the holy old man Simeon speaks to Mary and Joseph after they have presented the child Jesus. Taking the child in his arms, Simeon blesses God and, in chanting his hymn – the *Nunc Dimittis* -, acknowledges that God has revealed to him the Saving One, the Messiah, in the child he is holding in his arms. Simeon then turns to Mary; in his words to her, we are given a revelation central to the mystery of Mary: "This child is a sign of contradiction, set for the fall and the rise of many in Israel; and a sword will pierce your own soul, your own heart, that the thoughts of many hearts may be revealed" (Lk. 2:34-35). What "sword"? It is amazing how the Scriptures themselves always enlighten the Scriptures. If we know the Lukan gospel, we note that Jesus is shown throughout on the road to Jerusalem: already in the infancy gospel (Lk. 1-2), and then, in his public life, from Lk. 9:51 onwards with his face set decisively towards Jerusalem, Jesus climbs up, on his journey, dividing or sifting either individual persons or groups of persons, as a sharp "sword" would do –' dividing or sifting, that is, those who are his true authentic disciples from those who claim to be such but are so only in name, not in fact, at that real point of time.

Loss and Finding of the boy Jesus in the Temple (Lk. 2:41-52)
After three agonizing days of having lost their boy Jesus – God the Father had put Jesus in their charge – Mary and Joseph find him in the Temple. Then Mary's motherly heart voices her anguish and complaint: "Son, why have you done this to us? Your father (foster-father) and I have been looking anxiously for you". We are absolutely taken aback by the son Jesus' claim and seemingly intransigent reply: "How is it that you looked for me? Did you not know that I must be in the things that belong to my Father?" St. Luke, who will not hide or cover up anything, goes on quite honestly: "And they did not understand the words he spoke to them". Mary did not understand; but, as the Lukan account continues, "They went down to Nazareth, … and Mary kept all these words in her heart". She was too wise in the ways of God not to surmise that God was teaching her something. She allowed herself, 'seat of wisdom' that she was, to be instructed by God's Word. As if, she had said to herself, 'I do not understand, but God is teaching me something; so I must receive this Word of God and allow it to educate me'. Actively receiving God's Word; active receptivity and availability to the Word of God, this, as we have seen, is the core and heart of the mystery of Mary in the entire Lukan gospel.

Wedding Feast of Cana (Jn. 2:1-11)

In the Wedding Feast of Cana and the scene of the Crucifixion of Jesus (Jn. 19:25-27), Mary is called "Woman", the "Woman" of the mystery of Redemption. At Cana, Mary's maternal heart is quick to sense the embarrassment the wedding couple would face as the wine failed. She approaches her Son, and simply says: "They have no wine". To this, Jesus surprisingly remarks: "Woman, what does your concern have to do with me? My hour has not yet come!" "Woman" and "my hour": the "Woman" of the mystery of Redemption, and, in St. John's typical language, the "hour of Jesus" – the "hour" of Redemption. But there is even more about Mary's mystery in this Johannine passage. The very next words of Mary reveal her whole mystery: far from recoiling from what appears as 'rejection' of her intervention on behalf of the wedding couple, Mary says to the stewards of the feast: "Do whatever he tells you". Total availability to Jesus' word, to the Word of God! We note how eloquently Mary gives expression to her entire mystery. In point of fact, Mary is saying to us, to each and all of us: **"Do whatever he tells you!"** To each and all of us, Mary is saying: in this way, and only in this way, will you have *true and authentic devotion to me.* For this is, in a nutshell, the whole mystery of Mary: active and open availability to God's Word – to the Word of God that **is** Jesus Christ.

Mary at the foot of the Cross of Jesus (Jn. 19:25-27

At this peak moment of the "hour" of the mystery of Redemption, Mary is again called "Woman": "Woman, behold, your son!" Mary is the "Woman" most closely associated with Jesus **the** *"man"* of redemption, the unique Redeemer and Saviour. Mary is **not** a co-redeemer alongside Jesus; she is wholly on our side. She is redeemed like us, but she is the "first" (in honour and privilege) among the redeemed, because, as our representative on the wholly human side (the "Woman"), she collaborated actively in the actual objective working out of redemption. She actively received, in full openness and availability, the gift of redemption in her own person and life, and on behalf of all humankind – on behalf of each and all of us.

Conclusion

Inspired by the Word of God, we have seen Mary's entire mystery – her mystery in the mystery of Jesus Christ and in the mystery of the Church – wondrously summed up in her active openness and availability to God and His Word, expressed in her "Fiat": "Be it done to me according to your word". It is this attitude of her openness and availability in actively collaborating with the gift of redemption that makes her the open channel of this same gift of redemption for us. In this very attitude that sums up her whole mystery, Mary is held up as **type, figure, model and "icon" of the Church – that is, for all of us, who are the Church.**

To the extent, then, that we live out, in our daily Christian living, this attitude of active availability to God, His Word and His will – in which Mary is, as it were, personified – do we have true and genuine devotion to Mary, our Blessed Lady.

Herbert Alphonso SJ

4.6 The Church

Understand that the Church is a family.
Be aware that we belong to the Church.

What is the Church?

Starting Point
Think about the school as a community. In pairs, pupils could list the 'joys' and 'challenges' of belonging to the school.

Imagine you never went to school, what would it be like? Maybe your parents would educate you at home, but what would you miss out on?

- How does the Church family help us?
- What would we miss if we never went to Church?
- Why is it important to meet regularly with the Church family?

Explain that during the coming weeks we are going to explore many of the ways in which the family of the Church helps us to grow close to Jesus.

Explain: The Birth of the Church
Before ascending to heaven, Jesus gave his mission, power and authority to the apostles (Matt. 28:18-20).

At **Pentecost** when the Holy Spirit descended on the apostles, this marked the birth of the Church. The twelve apostles (Matthias was chosen to replace Judas Iscariot) were the first members of the Church because they had been the companions of Jesus. They heard all his teaching. They were witnesses of his miracles and his resurrection. Peter, as head of this Christian community, made decisions and governed the Church acting with the other apostles. They knew God was with them.

PPP: Pope Francis I

WS: Our Parish Church Project (TB & CD ROM).

Q. Why is the church in the middle of the picture on page 91? *(Because it is in church that we receive the sacraments that give us the grace and help necessary to go out and help others.)*

Research: pupils look at the parish website and newsletters to find out what happens and the help offered to people.

Discuss
Study a copy of the Apostles' Creed (TB page 91 & CD ROM). Where will you find the source for some of the beliefs in the Creed? For example:

"I believe in Jesus Christ ... born of the Virgin Mary". (Luke 2:7)

"I believe in Jesus Christ ... who was crucified, died and was buried". (Mark chapter 15)

"I believe in Jesus Christ ... who on the third day rose from the dead". (John 20:17-18)

The Sacraments

Understand that the Church is 'good news' for people.
Be aware that this 'good news' is also for us.

The Journey of Life

Note for teachers: The Church teaches that every spiritual soul is created immediately by God. It is, therefore, not 'produced' by the parents. It is also immortal. That means it does not perish when it separates from the body at death; it will be reunited with the body at the final Resurrection (CCC 364-366).

Starting point

Explain that life is a *little bit like a* journey and on the way there are some very important events that take place in our lives. See Pupil's Book pages 93-94.
Explain to pupils that there are two parts to us: our physical body and our spiritual life. We are made of body and soul.

- What would happen if we only had a meal once a week or once a month?
- So what do you think happens to our spiritual life if we only pray to Jesus about once a week or less frequently?

Now we are going to learn about the help that the Church offers us on our journey through life.

Additional activities

1. Draw an outline of a long road. For each sacrament you have received or will receive later in life, put a little church at the side of the road. Explain what happened or will happen when you receive a sacrament.
See Book 3 for help with the Sacraments of Baptism, Reconciliation and the Eucharist.

2. Choose two sacraments. Explain how they can help a person to live a good life.
*(For example: when we fail to love others as God asked and we want to make things right with God and others we can receive the **Sacrament of Reconciliation**. In this Sacrament we can be certain that because God loves us so much, He forgives us for all the wrong things we have done and He offers us a special grace to help us love others. In the **Eucharist**, which we frequently call the Mass, when we take an active part in it we are able to offer ourselves in love with Jesus to the Father, we receive Jesus in Holy Communion and get the strength to be able to love all our brothers and sisters in the world.)*

Plenary

- How many sacraments are there?
- Why do we say that they will help us on our journey through life?
- Who can give examples of how a sacrament will help us?

Song: 'God's Greatest Gift' (CD Share the Light by Bernadette Farrell).

The Church's Year

Know about the different seasons in the Church's year.
Think about why these times are important for us.

The Liturgical Year

Starting point
- What season are we in now? *(Summer)*
- What are the other seasons in the year?
- What happens in nature during each season?
- Does anyone know about the seasons in the Church's year?
  Build on what pupils already know.

Discussion to enable pupils to

a) explain what they know of the Church's seasons.
   What do we prepare for in Advent?
   What happens at Christmas?
   What is Lent? Why do we have the Season of Lent?
   What happens at Easter?
   What very big feast comes at the end of the Easter Season?
   What happens in Ordinary Time?

b) Make links between one or two of the Liturgical Seasons and the devotional
   practices. *(For example, in Lent we make the Stations of the Cross, especially on Good Friday; in
   Advent we have an Advent Wreath and say special prayers; at Christmas we have a crib.)*

 SMART notebook: 'The Church's Year'.

 PPP: Vestments in Church

 Additional activities
1. Imagine your parish church was burnt down during the night.
   a) What do you think the newspapers would be able to say about the people
      who belonged to it?
   b) How do you think it might affect you and your family?

2. Think of someone you know or heard about who has great faith and trust in God.
   How would other people know that this person had great faith and trust in God by
   what he or she does? *(Discussion prior to setting the task: what does the person do to help others; how
   do you know they have faith and trust in God? Do they go to church? Do they pray, etc.?)*

 SMART notebook: Glossary

The Communion of Saints

Know about the Communion of Saints and the Holy Souls.
Be aware of how they can help us.

What is the Communion of Saints?

Notes for Teachers: Someone who dies in God's grace (and therefore at peace with God and men) but who still needs purification before he/she can see God face to face is in purgatory (cf. CCC1030-1031). We can help the souls in purgatory through our fasting, prayers and good works but especially through celebration of the Mass.

 Starting point

Explain that the "communion of saints" is made up of all people who place their hope in Jesus and belong to him through Baptism. It includes those who have already died and those still alive (cf. CCC946-962).

The good news is that we can ask those who have already died to help us and we can help them by our prayers.

Invite pupils to study the illustration on page 98.
- Who do you see in it?
- Where do you think the saints are?
- Where are the souls in purgatory? Why do you think the artist has painted them in purple? Which liturgical seasons are shown in purple on page 95? Why?

Feast of All Saints – 1st November.
Feast of the Holy Souls - 2nd November.

 Additional Activities

1. **Hymn: For all the Saints**
   Pupils re-write this first verse of the hymn in their own words and explain what it means.

   > "For all the saints who from their labours rest,
   > who thee by faith before the world confessed,
   > thy name O Jesus be for ever blest."

2. Watch the **PPP: St. Thérèse of Lisieux** (CD ROM).
   Discuss:
   a) Why do you think so many people in Britain came to be near her relics?
   b) In what ways do you think this might have made a difference to their lives?

3. "I will spend my heaven doing good upon the earth" St. Thérèse of Lisieux
   Think about these words of St. Thérèse.
   How does she help us to understand the 'Communion of Saints'?

The Mission of the Church

Know about God's call to individuals.
Reflect on their responses.

Jesus passes on his Mission

Starting point

Explain that when the Holy Spirit came upon the apostles, the crowds of people who heard them preach on the teaching of Jesus and the fact that he had risen from the dead, were so impressed that three thousand were converted the first day. The number of Christians rapidly increased. One of the reasons for this was that St. Paul completely changed his whole life after Jesus appeared to him on the road to Damascus. Before that, he was a very powerful Pharisee bent on persecuting the Christians. But almost from the moment Jesus appeared to him, he no longer persecuted the Christians but joined them. He became the most important missionary in the history of the Church.

However, most of the work of spreading the Good News of Jesus was done by **ordinary people** whose everyday work brought them into contact with people who had not heard the Gospel. People could see Christians being very thoughtful and kind to everyone and would say to each other, "See how these Christians love one another".

PPP: A Missionary Sister
PPP: The Mission of the Columban Sisters

Additional Activity: Be a Missionary!

In the Sacrament of Baptism we have received the Spirit of Jesus, the Holy Spirit, so now we have to be his witnesses. That means we have to pass on the Good News about Jesus.
All important aspects of the life of Jesus should be covered.
For example,

- His birth and flight into Egypt
- Miracles and what they revealed about Jesus;
- Parables and the important messages in them;
- Jesus true God and true man;
- Passion, Death and Resurrection;
- Ascension, Pentecost and birth of the Church.

You can work in pairs and witness to the teaching of Jesus by:
- a speech to give at a school assembly;
- an article for a school newsletter;
- a webpage for the school website;
- a poster that you could take home to your family;
- an article for the school notice board;
- inviting your parents in to school for your presentations;
- any other ideas of your own.

Mary, Mother of the Church

Deepen our understanding of Mary.
Reflect on how she can help all of us.

What do we know about Mary?

 ### Starting point
Explain that Mary, being the Mother of Jesus, is also our Mother. Mary like a good mother will always stand up for us and be ready to help us if we pray earnestly to her. Her love for us will never cease.

 ### PPP: Feast Days of Mary

1st January	Mary, Mother of God	21st August	Our Lady of Knock
11th February	Our Lady of Lourdes	8th September	Birthday of Our Lady
25th March	Annunciation	15th September	Our Lady of Sorrows
13th May	Our Lady of Fatima	24th September	Our Lady of
31st May	Visitation		Walsingham
15th August	Assumption of Our	7th October	Our Lady of the Rosary
	Lady into heaven	8th December	Immaculate
22nd August	Coronation of Our		Conception
	Lady	12th December	Our Lady of Guadalupe

 ### Additional Activity
Work in pairs. Choose a feast of Our Lady. Design a page for a Class Book on Mary, Our Mother.

The Rosary:
There are twenty decades to the Rosary. These will be covered in detail in Book 5; it is sufficient just to mention that in the tradition of the Church many Catholics say five decades of the rosary daily. For example:

 ### PPP: The Joyful Mysteries of the Rosary
- The Annunciation (Lk. 1:26-38)
- The Visitation (Lk. 1:39-45)
- The Birth of our Lord (Lk. 2:1-7)
- The Presentation (Lk. 2:21-24)
- The Finding in the Temple (Lk. 2:41-50)

 ### Additional Activity
Choose one of the Joyful Mysteries of the Rosary.
Give details to show how the source of the Mystery is found in the Gospel.

The Apostles' Creed

I believe in God,

the Father almighty,

Creator of heaven and earth

and in Jesus Christ, His only Son, our Lord,

who was conceived by the Holy Spirit,

born of the Virgin Mary,

suffered under Pontius Pilate,

was crucified, died and was buried;

he descended into hell;

on the third day he rose again from the dead;

he ascended into heaven,

and is seated at the right hand of God the Father almighty;

from there he will come to judge the living and the dead.

I believe in the Holy Spirit,

the holy catholic Church,

the communion of saints,

the forgiveness of sins,

the resurrection of the body,

and the life everlasting,

Amen.

Our Parish Church Project

The aim of this project is to train you to act as a guide for your Parish Church. It may happen that people of other faiths will request a guided tour. Also, it will give you the opportunity to introduce other pupils in your class to your church.

Plan

- You could work in Parish Groups.

- You are asked to prepare a talk about your Church and all the different things in it: - name of Church, altar, tabernacle, lectern, priest's chair, baptistery, crucifix, statues and stained glass windows.

- You will need to prepare visual aids to help you with your talk - you may use drawings, sketches, photos or a video.

- You will need to appoint a group leader who will make sure that everybody in the group has an important task to do. Set deadlines for these tasks to be done.

- Every member of the group will need to visit the Parish Church in order to see all the things he/she has to speak or write about.

- If you need more information, you may wish to speak to one of the priests in the Parish. Please be sure to telephone first to make an appointment to see him.

Assessment of Project
- Discuss with your teacher how marks will be awarded.
- Extra marks will be given for imaginative presentation, including use of computer, camera, video camera etc.

Our Parish Church

Here are some questions you need to be able to answer.

Why is there an altar?
It is a table on which the bread and wine are changed into the body and blood of Jesus during Mass.
It is the place where the sacrifice of Jesus is made present for us.

Why is there a lectern?
A lectern is a sign of the importance we give to the Bible: the Word of God.

Why does the priest have a special chair?
The priest represents Jesus, so he has an important seat.
He sits down to listen to the readings from the Bible and to pray silently.

Why is there a tabernacle?
After Mass the consecrated Hosts, which we call the Blessed Sacrament, are kept in the tabernacle. Many people wish to pray privately in front of the Blessed Sacrament in our churches.

Why is there a crucifix?
The crucifix reminds us of the death of Jesus on the cross.

Why do people genuflect when they go into church?
They genuflect out of respect for the presence of Jesus in the Blessed Sacrament in the tabernacle.

Why are there Stations of the Cross around the walls of the church?
Many people reflect on each Station of the Cross particularly during Lent. They meditate on what Jesus has suffered for us and pray to him.

Assessment

The purpose of assessment is for teachers to know and understand what pupils can do and then to use this information for future planning. It should also help teachers to:

- identify pupils requiring special assistance and those who are ready for more challenging tasks;
- evaluate their own teaching and, if necessary, highlight their need for adequate preparation and planning.

Good Assessment should have variety, flexibility and be based on the professional judgement of teachers.

Assessment is most effective when it provides pupils with a clear understanding of their attainment, that is, their strengths and weaknesses and what they need to do to improve.

Assessment tasks are best integrated into lessons. This encourages pupils to take increasing responsibility for their progress.

It is recommended that teachers identify the tasks they will use for assessment at the beginning of the term and **do the task themselves first.**

Levels of Attainment

The Levels of Attainment are based on the Bishop's Conference Guidance for England & Wales. The overview on page 95 offers guidance on using the 'Levels' with the Pupil's Book 4.

National Expectation

Range of levels within which the majority of pupils are expected to work.	Expected attainment for the majority of pupils at the end of the key stage.
Key Stage One Level 1 - 3	At the age of 7 Level 2
Key Stage Two Level 2 - 5	At the age of 11 Level 4

Overview of Levels

AT 1 Learning ABOUT the Catholic Faith (i), (ii) & (iii)

AT2 Learning FROM the Catholic Faith (i) & (ii)

Strand Level	i) Beliefs, teachings and sources	ii) celebration & ritual	iii) social & moral practices & way of life	i) engagement with own & others' beliefs & values	ii) engagement with questions of meaning & purpose
1	Briefly tell a story	Recognise some religious signs and symbols and use some religious words	Be able to say why it is important to: learn about Jesus; say sorry, etc.	Talk about their own experiences and feelings	Say what they wonder about
2	Tell a story and say what is important about it	Use phrases to describe religious actions and symbols	What are some of the things Christians do?	Ask and respond to questions about their own and others' experiences and feelings.	Ask questions about what they and others wonder about and realise that some of these are difficult to answer
3	Make links between the story and the message it gives	What are some of the big events Christians celebrate?	Give reasons for certain actions by believers; Make links between belief and practice	Make links to show how feeling and beliefs affect their behaviour and that of others	Compare their own and other people's ideas about questions that are difficult to answer
4	Describe and show understanding of religious sources, beliefs, ideas, feelings and experiences, making links between them	Use religious terms to show understanding of different liturgies, e.g. the Mass, Sacrament of Reconciliation	Show understanding of how religious belief shapes life	Show how own and others' decisions are informed by beliefs and values	Engage with and respond to questions of life in the light of religious teaching
5	Identify sources of religious belief and explain how distinctive religious beliefs arise	Describe and explain the meaning and purpose of a variety of forms of worship	Identify similarities and differences between peoples' responses to social and moral values and behaviour	Explain what beliefs and values inspire and influence them and others	Demonstrate how religious beliefs and teaching give some explanation of the purpose and meaning of human life

4.1 The Bible

1. How did Abraham's belief in God change his life?
   You need to include:
   - what God asked of him;
   - details of what Abraham did;
   - how he helped strangers;
   - how Abraham and Sarah were rewarded by God.   [AT1 L3 (iii)]

2. a) How might the account of how Moses helped the Israelites
      escape from Egypt help us to believe that God will always keep
      His promise?   [AT1 L3 (i)]

   b) Explain how our Church still recalls these events?
      Think about:
      - the readings in church or
      - community or private prayer.   [AT1 L4 (i)]

3. a) Briefly tell the story of David and Goliath (1Sam. 17:32-52).
   b) What does this account tell us about David?
   c) What does it tell us about God?
   d) How might this Scripture text be used at Mass?   [AT1 L3 (i)]
   e) How might this Scripture text help people who have to face
      big difficulties? Give examples.   [AT2 L3-4 (ii)]

4. a) Choose one reading from the Old Testament.
   b) Write a summary of it in your own words.   [AT1 L2 (i)]
   c) Explain how this reading could be used at Mass.
   d) Why do you think this reading is important?
      Who might it help?   [AT1 L3 (iii)]

4.2 Trust in God

1. Imagine your friend is very worried about something that is going to happen.
   a) How would you help your friend to trust in God?
   b) Can you explain to him or her some important points to remember about trusting in God?
   c) Give examples of how others learned to trust in God.   [AT2 L3 (i)]

2. a) In what ways did Mary trust in God?   [AT1 L2 (i)]
      Think about
      • Annunciation
      • Birth of Jesus
      • Flight into Egypt
   b) How did her trust in God change her life?
      Think about the mystery of the Incarnation.   [AT1 L4 (iii)]

3. The Church teaches that there are three persons in one God.
   a) What is this mystery called?
   b) What are the names of the three persons?   [AT1 L2 (i)]
   c) Briefly explain what the Bible tells us about each of them?
   d) What prayer do we say in honour of the three persons in one God?
                                                          [AT1 L3 (i)]

4. a) In your own words, give a short account of what happened at the
      (i) Annunciation (Lk. 1:26-38)
      (ii) Visitation (Lk. 1:39-45)   [AT1 L2 (i)]

   b) Can you explain how these accounts from the Gospel of Luke help us to understand the first part of the 'Hail Mary'?
                                                          [AT1 L3 (i)]

4.3 Jesus, the Teacher

1. a) What is a parable?
   b) In the Parable of the Sower, what does the seed represent?
   c) Describe what happened to the seed that fell in two of the following places:
      • on the edge of the path;
      • on a path;
      • among thorns;
      • good soil.
   d) Explain why that happened to those seeds.
   e) What can we learn from these examples?   [AT1 L3 (i)]

2. Read the parable of 'The Unforgiving Servant' (Matt. 18:23-35).
   a) Who do you think is most like God in this parable?
   b) What was the lesson that Jesus wanted the people to understand from this parable?
   c) How can we live out the message of this parable?   [AT2 L3-4 (i)]

3. a) Study the Beatitudes. Choose two that you believe help you to live a good life.
      • Give examples of what you do.
      • Explain why you do it.   [AT1 L3 (iii)]
   b) Choose two more Beatitudes that you have seen someone else live out in his or her life.
      • Give examples of what this person does.
      • Why you think their beliefs influence their way of life.
                                                            [AT2 L3-4 (i)]

4. Jesus came to show us the way to live.
   a) Write three important things that Jesus teaches about the way we should live our lives.
   b) Give an example of a person who because of his or her belief in the teaching of Jesus, does certain things.
   c) Give an example of something you do because of your belief in the teaching of Jesus.   [AT1 L4 (iii)]

4.4 Jesus, the Saviour

1. The Church teaches that Jesus is truly God and as man truly human. What evidence is there in the Bible to support this belief?
   Include
   - what made Jesus truly human;
   - what he did that shows he is truly God.   [AT1 L3 (i)]

2. a) Explain what happened at the first Passover.
   b) How did Jesus give a new meaning to the Passover?   [AT1 L3 (i)]
   c) What happened over 2,000 years ago is made present every day at Mass in Church.
      What are the links between the Last Supper and the Mass (Eucharist)?   [AT1 L4 (i)]

3. On Good Friday, after Jesus had been taken away by the guards, Peter was scared in case he would be arrested. He was asked if he was a follower of Jesus and he said he did not even know him.

   If you had met Peter after he heard the cock crow
   a) what would you have said to him?
   b) how would you have tried to help him?
   c) what do you think Jesus would say to him when he met him again?
      You need to refer to some of the things Jesus said, for example,

   Use your Bible.
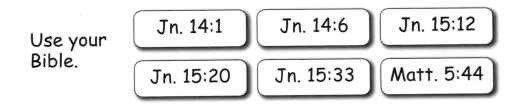
   | Jn. 14:1 | Jn. 14:6 | Jn. 15:12 |
   | Jn. 15:20 | Jn. 15:33 | Matt. 5:44 |

   [AT2 L4 (ii)]

4. On Easter Sunday, we celebrate the resurrection of Jesus from the dead.
   What does the resurrection of Jesus mean for you?
   How will it affect the way you live your life?   [AT1 L4 (iii)]

4.5 The Early Christians

1. In what ways did Stephen's belief in Jesus shape his life?
   Think about his:
   - courage;
   - vision;
   - faithfulness;
   - and what it was that identified him most of all with Jesus at the hour of his death.   [AT1 L3-4 (iii)]

2. a) Briefly retell what you know about Saul on the road to Damascus?
                                                        [AT1 L2 (i)]
   b) Explain why Jesus said, 'Saul, Saul, why are you persecuting me'?
   c) What is the link between what Jesus said to Saul and the reason why we should try to be kind and helpful to everyone?
                                                        [AT1 L3 (i)]

3. Paul became one of the greatest apostles in the Church.
   Give examples of how his experience on the road to Damascus shaped his future life.
   Think about:
   - his writings;
   - what he did and said.   [AT1 L4 (iii)]

4. a) From your study of Paul, give examples of ways in which his teaching has influenced your life.
      Think about 1 Cor. 13:4-7 and Col. 3:12-13.
   b) In what ways do you think Paul's experience has helped other people you know or hear about? Give examples.
                                                        [AT2 L4 (i)]

4.6 The Church

1. Imagine some inspectors are visiting the school. They know it is a Catholic school and they want to find out from the pupils what Catholics believe. In order to help them write down
   a) what Catholics believe about Jesus;
   b) where we find evidence for these beliefs.   [AT1 L4 (i)]

2. a) Take one statement from the Apostles' Creed. Explain it.
   b) Find evidence in the Bible to support it. Quote the reference.
   c) Which sacrament do we have in which the Creed is said by everyone present?   [AT1 L4 (i)]

3. a Name two liturgical seasons.
   b) Explain their importance.   [AT1 L3 (ii)]
   c) Which do you think is the most important season in the Church's year? Give reasons for your answer.   [AT2 L4 (ii)]

4. Imagine you are preparing to go as a missionary to a country where people have never heard about God.
   a) Choose to go as a teacher, a doctor, a nurse, a priest or a nun. Give reasons for your choice.
   b) Use bullet points to plan what you will teach the people when you get there.
   c) Explain **why** would you want to teach these things?
                    [AT2 L4 (ii)]

Guidance on Levels of Achievement Tasks

4.1 The Bible

1. For Level 3 all the points need to be included see PB pp. 8-10. [AT1 L3 (iii)]

2. a) Pupils need to make link with the text see PB pp.18-20. [AT1 L3 (i)]
   b) For help see
   - TB WS 'How the Bible is used at Mass p.21;
   - WS CD ROM 'The Hymn of Victory' Ex. 15;
   - PPPs 'The Bible and the Divine Office'
     'Jewish worship of God – Passover' on CD Rom 4. [AT1 L4 (i)]

3. Questions a) – d) PB p. 21 and TB WS p. 21 [AT1 L3 (i)]
   Question e) Discussion should already have taken place in class about a variety of big challenges some people have to face. [AT2 L3-4 (ii)]

4. a) – b) A short summary is all that is required.
   c) – d) TB WS p. 21 pupils need to able to give a good answer with an example.
   [AT1 L3 (iii)]

4.2 Trust in God

1. See PB p. 26 for important points which need to be included. [AT2 L3 (i)]

2. Pupils need to mention the Annunciation, Birth of Jesus, flight into Egypt and mystery of the Incarnation for L4. [AT1 L4 (iii)]

3. c) See PB page 38;
   d) 'Glory be to the Father ...' or 'In the name of the Father ...'

4. b) 'Hail Mary ..." is the angel greeting Mary.
   'Blessed art thou among women ..." is what Elizabeth said to Mary.
   [AT1 L3 (i)]

4.3 Jesus, the Teacher

1. a) A parable is an earthly story with a heavenly meaning.
   b) The seed represents the word of God (the teaching of Jesus).
   c) The meanings are in the PB p. 55.
   d) For explanations read Luke 8:9-15.
   * Those on the edge of the path easily give in to temptations.
   * Those on the rock welcome the teaching of Jesus at first, but when life is difficult they easily give up believing in it.
   * Those that fell among thorns easily forget the teaching of Jesus when they have worries or lots of good things.
   * Those on good soil hear the word of God(teaching of Jesus), believe it and live it out in their daily life.
   e) For example: for good seed we learn that it is important to live out the teaching of Jesus by doing good deeds.   [AT1 L4 (iii)]

4.4 Jesus, the Saviour

1. Pupils need to include the examples given in PB pp. 58 & 60 or others.
                                                              [AT1 L4 (i)]

2. a) See PB p. 18.
   b) See PB pp. 64-65 and CD ROM 4 PPP 'Meaning of the Last Supper'.
   c) For revision see TB WS p. 64.   [AT1 L4 (i)]

3. See PB p. 67 for discussion prior to setting the task.
   For a Level 4 pupils need to be able to
   make links with the teaching of Jesus, e.g. Jn. 14:1; Jn. 14:6; Jn. 15:12; Jn.15:20; Jn. 16:33; Matt. 5:44   [AT2 L4 (ii)]

4. What does the resurrection of Jesus mean? See PB p. 73.
   How will it affect the way you live your life? Pupils need to include examples of how they 'live out' the teaching of Jesus and mention that they continually entrust their lives to him.   [AT1 L4 (iii)]

4.5 The Early Christians

1. Stephen had the courage to challenge those who did not believe in Jesus and to speak the truth about Jesus. See page PB p. 79 and TB WS p. 78.
   He had vision to see how the Old Testament prophecies were fulfilled in Jesus.
   He was willing to die for his faith in Jesus.
   He was like Jesus in the way he forgave those who stoned him.

   [AT1 L3-4 (iii)]

2. b) & c) Revise PB pp. 51-52 where Jesus explains that what we do to others we do to him.   [AT1 L3 (i)]

3. Revise Paul's mission PB p. 85-87; quotations from his writings PB p. 89 also Gal. 5:22-23.   [AT1 L4)iii)]

4. Pupils give examples from their own and lives of others based on how the writings and example of Paul have influenced them. They need to refer to 1Cor: 13:4-7 and Col. 3:12-13.   [AT2 L4 (i)]

4.6 The Church

1. Pupils should be able to draw on their knowledge of the Bible and belief in the Apostles' Creed, TB p. 91. Pupils need to mention both sources in order to get a Level 4.   [AT1 L4 (i)]

2. Statement from the Apostles' Creed TB. P. 91
   In the Sunday Mass (Sacrament of the Eucharist) the Creed is said by everyone.
   [AT1 L4 (i)]

3. Liturgical Seasons PB p. 95; for their importance see p. 97
   To get a Level 4 pupils need to be able to explain in depth why their chosen 'Season' is the most important. For revision discuss the real meaning of the Incarnation and the passion, death and resurrection of Jesus. Reference to these will enable pupils to reach a Level 4.   [AT2 L4 (ii)]

4. For b) and c) pupils need to be able to focus on the Bible, the teaching of Jesus and his mission, also the essential teaching of the Church, i.e. the Creed and be able to give reasons for their importance.   [AT2 L4 (ii)]